W9-AFA-155

DOGS OF COURAGE

 This Large Print Book carries the
Seal of Approval of N.A.V.H.

DOGS OF COURAGE

STORIES OF SERVICE DOGS, POLICE DOGS, THERAPY DOGS, AND OTHER HEROIC DOGS FROM AROUND THE WORLD

LISA ROGAK

THORNDIKE PRESS
A part of Gale, Cengage Learning

GALE
CENGAGE Learning·

Detroit • New York • San Francisco • New Haven, Conn • Waterville, Maine • London

Copyright © 2012 by Lisa Rogak.
Thorndike Press, a part of Gale, Cengage Learning.

ALL RIGHTS RESERVED
Thorndike Press® Large Print Inspirational.
The text of this Large Print edition is unabridged.
Other aspects of the book may vary from the original edition.
Set in 16 pt. Plantin.

LIBRARY OF CONGRESS CATALOGING-IN-PUBLICATION DATA

Library of Congress CIP DATA on file. Cataloguing in Publication Data for this book is available from the Library of Congress
ISBN-13:978-1-4104-5482-9 (hardcover)
ISBN-10: 1-4104-5482-7 (hardcover)

Published in 2013 by arrangement with St. Martin's Press, LLC

Printed in the United States of America
1 2 3 4 5 6 7 17 16 15 14 13

For Cheryl Trotta and her dog-tourage,
where there's never a dull moment . . .

CONTENTS

INTRODUCTION

According to a survey conducted in 2011 by the American Pet Products Association, there are approximately 78.2 million owned dogs in the United States. Australia has one of the highest rates of dog ownership in the world; the Australian Companion Animal Council reported in 2009 that 36 percent of households in the country contained at least one dog.

The same holds true throughout the world: the European Pet Food Industry Federation estimates that 27 percent of households in the European Union own at least one dog, resulting in a whopping sixty million canines across the continent. And in Japan, where pet ownership didn't start to gain a toehold until the 1990s, there are now roughly eighteen million dogs, and they've become so popular that one pet food company even pays its dog-owning employees the equivalent of $10 a month to put toward canine expenses.

And every one of them has the potential to be a Dog of Courage, regardless of breed, particular talent, or size. While every canine has the ability to touch a human life — whether it's a much-loved family pet or a stranger's dog who helps to lift the spirits with just a friendly glance or wag of the tail — a Dog of Courage works hard to help people in a wide variety of ways. You see, at this very minute, there are thousands of dogs being trained to perform tasks to directly benefit the humans around them, whether they've been bonded together for years or have just met. A Dog of Courage can save a man from almost certain death after an avalanche devastates a mountain community or make it possible for a veteran crippled by PTSD to feel comfortable and secure enough to venture out in public again. These hardworking dogs are a major part of the lives of people all over the world, much more than even most dog lovers recognize. They become Dogs of Courage simply by doing the job they've been trained to do, which in most cases happens to be a job they love with all their heart.

Dogs of Courage come in all shapes and sizes and range from being highly trained to never setting foot in an obedience class. At the most basic level, their heroic natures stem from acting upon deeply innate instincts. Regardless of their backgrounds, and whether they're purebred or made up of more breeds than you can count on the fingers of one paw, man's best friend will go above and beyond the call of duty to help the people he loves — as well as those he's never met before — in some very surprising ways.

We are always heartened when we hear stories of Dogs of Courage in the news; they make us feel good in an era of pessimism, amid an overabundance of bad-news headlines. But while we smile at the story of a dog who saved a couple of three-week-old kittens abandoned by the side of a busy road and left to die, or the two-legged dog who hops through hospital wards, inspiring paraplegics and others who struggle with devastating disabilities, we don't often hear about the *why* and the *how*.

Why do dogs go out of their way to help us, often in situations that place them in danger and that may prove risky to their own health and welfare? And for those who are highly trained — like a German shepherd trained in police work who chases after and catches a bad guy without once touching him, or a beagle who can sniff out laboratory specimens in test tubes that contain cancer cells — *how* do they get that way? How are dogs able to perform tasks and work in tandem with the

11

humans who are their partners?

Dogs of Courage answers these questions and many more. I shine a spotlight on heroic canines not only around the world but also throughout history. Through their stories, you'll learn how arson dogs can sniff out a minute particle of flammable liquid that is all but invisible not only to human detectives but also to high-tech equipment. You'll discover the remarkable ability of search-and-rescue dogs who can pick up a trail and scent of a person that is weeks, perhaps even months, old.

You may be surprised to learn that Dogs of Courage can be supreme multitaskers. Indeed, many of the dogs profiled in this book could rightfully be featured in more than one chapter. For instance, diabetic- and allergy-alert dogs could also be considered guide, service, and assistance dogs. However, because there is so much going on in the medical field that uses canines in research and in helping people, I had more than enough information to devote an entire chapter to Dogs of Courage who work as medical detectives.

And when it comes to guide and service dogs, in addition to helping their owners to navigate their way through daily life despite having severe physical disabilities, these dogs also provided them with much-valued therapy; thus, they could have been included in the therapy dog chapter. But instead I feature them in their own chapter.

Though stories of dogs from all corners of the globe are detailed in each chapter, sometimes there's one particular dog who deserves a spotlight all his or her own. And so scattered throughout each chapter are profiles of dogs whose stories are incredibly poignant, heartwarming, and inspirational.

Why are we drawn in by these stories of Dogs of Courage? The answer is simple: Both humans and canines are essentially cut from the same cloth. "The dog thinks, feels, and reacts in ways very much like humans, which explains its unique ability to fit into human society," says Bonnie Bergin, the founder of Canine Companions for Independence, the first organization in the United States formed specifically to train service dogs. "The plasticity, the versatility, the adaptability of the canine species is very much aligned with ours. . . . No animal does more for us, none share a more intimate relationship with us, nor can any claim more years of alliance with us than the dog — our partner, our friend, our helpmate."

There have been literally millions of stories about Dogs of Courage handed down through the years, and narrowing them down to fit into the pages of a book presented frequent challenges. I chose the ones I thought best exemplified the nature of the canine spirit: loving, loyal, and operating on pure instinct. Some of the stories will make you cry, while others will have you laughing at a dog's foibles. After all, dogs don't care how they look when they're doing what's in their nature. We could all learn from these Dogs of Courage and apply some small fraction of their philosophies to our own lives.

Perhaps John Grogan, author of the mega–best seller *Marley & Me,* puts it best when it comes to why dogs touch our hearts in such a unique fashion: "People can learn a lot from their dogs. Lessons on how to lead happier, more fulfilling lives. Lessons for successful relationships. Think about it. Many of the qualities that come so effortlessly to dogs — loyalty, devotion, selflessness, unflagging optimism, unqualified love — can be elusive to humans. My hunch is that people who act more like dogs have happier marriages."

It's no wonder that so many people all over the world want a dog of their very own. Louis Sabin, the author of numerous books for young people, may have captured most succinctly why we all want a dog in our lives: "No matter how little money and how few possessions you own, having a dog makes you rich."

CHAPTER ONE:
DOGS OF COURAGE

On January 20, 2012, the U.S. Post Office unveiled a new series of stamps to honor a very special kind of canine: the working dog. To some people, they're also known as Dogs of Courage.

From guide dogs for the blind to search-and-rescue dogs working at Ground Zero in lower Manhattan, the dogs featured on the new "Dogs at Work" series of stamps have countless chances each day to show their courage, not only to their handlers but also to any human they encounter. The sheets of 65¢ stamps show four different kinds of Dogs of Courage just doing their jobs: a military working dog, a guide dog assisting a blind owner, a therapy dog, and a search-and-rescue dog.

"We are proud to commemorate these specialized dogs on stamps," said U.S. Postal Inspection Service Homeland Security Coordinator Michael T. Butler in announcing the stamps. "These animals are critical to serving individuals with special needs and critical to enabling successful rescues."[1]

The postal service printed eighty million sheets of the stamps, and many dog lovers said it's about time that these courageous dogs were recognized for their service.

Dogs are born with courage. It's up to the humans who surround them to draw it out of them and finesse it in a way that benefits dog, human, and society as a whole.

WHAT IS A DOG OF COURAGE?

Dogs of Courage are many things. Tucker, a black Lab, works alongside researchers in the Pacific Northwest to help determine the cause of a significant decrease in the orca whale population. Magellan and Moses patiently work regular stints as therapy dogs in an elementary school classroom in San Marcos, Texas, to help children strengthen their reading skills when they read books aloud to the seemingly attentive canines.

There's also Fagan, a Czech shepherd who spent eleven of his thirteen years sniffing out narcotics and chasing after bad guys with the Southaven Police Department in Memphis, Tennessee, alongside his human partners. "He was absolutely fearless," said department chief Steve Pirtle. "Fagan was truly a working dog and he loved to work."[2]

Captain Wayne Perkins, who served as the commander of Southaven's K-9 Division, worked alongside Fagan for most of the dog's tenure. His colleague, Lieutenant Mark Little, tells a story that exemplified Fagan's bravery. "We had one pursuit that raced into Memphis, where the driver bailed out and ran into some woods," Little said. As the car's other passenger also fled the scene, "Perkins released Fagan, who followed the suspect into the woods, found him and then brought him back out of the woods. As Fagan got the driver, the driver hit him in the head, but after a few minutes of recovery time, Perkins then released the dog on the trail of the passenger in the vehicle. Fagan tracked the passenger to an apartment house about 100 yards away. He made both catches on the same case even though he had been hit."

"The only term that comes to mind is 'countless,'" said Pirtle about the number of officer injuries — even possible deaths — that Fagan had likely prevented. "We always said that if we could have taught Fagan how to drive, his handlers would have been out of jobs. He was just that good."[3]

At the same time, a Dog of Courage could be a Hollywood dog from the 1930s who was heroic because he served as the bright spot in the day of millions of people who had the misfortune to live during the Depression.

But many more Dogs of Courage go unnoticed to all but their human companions. Their courage and valor are smaller and quieter, but no less important.

Of course, anyone who has spent any amount of time with a dog — especially one who's been abandoned and unwanted — already knows that while he may feel that he's the one saving the dog, in most cases the dog is actually saving him.

Case in point: David James Knowles from Oak Brook, Illinois, adopted Lucy, a Lab and whippet mix barely six months old with a surfeit of energy. He realized he had his work cut out for him.

Considered to be unadoptable because of her nonstop curiosity and motion, Lucy required patient training. Knowles had no way of knowing that he and Lucy had begun an eighteen-year relationship that would forever change his life.

"Life is about the simple details," Knowles said. "The simple details are what dogs understand. That's what they convey to us — the simple details for genuine quality life."[4]

And so that's how Knowles approached training the dog. But the changes Lucy would bring to his own life would turn out to be profound. You see, at over three hundred pounds, Knowles ignored his own health while he doted on his canine companion.

It took a crisis to turn everything around. In July 2000, Lucy was diagnosed with cancer, and it served as a wake-up call for Knowles. He knew that his remaining time with her was extremely limited, but while others might have used the excuse of the loss of their best friend to wallow in self-pity — not to mention food — Knowles was inspired.

In an effort to boost Lucy's precarious health, the two began to take long walks around the neighborhood before venturing farther afield to nearby parks and forests, something that was new to the both of them. Knowles also learned about good nutrition and began to eat better.

To his delight, Knowles began to lose weight. By the time Lucy succumbed to the cancer, he had lost sixty pounds. Knowles was of course devastated, but he continued to work on his lifestyle changes, and by the end of 2001, he had lost close to half his body weight. He wrote *Lucy's Lessons: Thirteen Lessons to Help You Find Joy and Happiness in Your Life,* in which he detailed their history together in the form of the life philosophies that Lucy had taught him through the years.

"The lesson here is not about my weight loss," said Knowles. "Your pets want to get out and enjoy life, they want to exercise, and maybe that's a lesson for people. All of the lessons are intertwined with each other. My lifestyle changed, and that allowed me to understand the lessons she was giving me."[5]

Indeed, Marjorie Garber, in her groundbreaking book *Dog Love,* writes that "the dog becomes the repository of those model human properties that we have cynically ceased to find among humans. Where today can we find the full panoply of William Bennett's *Book of Virtues* — from Courage and Responsibility to Loyalty and Family Values — but in Lassie and Beethoven and Millie and Checkers and Spot?"[6]

It's no wonder that humans look up to dogs. After all, they embody many traits that people aspire to — and often fail at. This makes perfect sense, because the truth is that when it comes to people and dogs, we're not really too far apart. According to gene-mapping research, humans and dogs share about 75 percent of their DNA.

"Working dogs often act as human surrogates and share many capacities with humans," writes William S. Helton in *Canine Ergonomics*. "Dogs, like humans, are products of uncontrolled evolution — they were not built with a purpose in mind. Dogs, unlike machines, do jobs roughly the way humans do. . . . Dogs, like humans and entirely unlike machines, are flexible. No machine in existence can replicate all the tasks a dog can be trained to do. Like people, dogs cannot really be forced to work; they must be persuaded, encouraged, threatened, or enticed and the possibility of a revolt is always present."[7]

There have been Dogs of Courage as long as humans have had canines as their companions and their coworkers. "Dogs are sharers in human fortunes and have been since the Mesolithic Era," said Diana Schaub, professor and chairman of the Department of Political Science at Loyola College in Maryland. "Whether in times of rising or falling civilization, dogs share not only our lot but also many of our virtues and vices."[8]

But contrary to popular sentiment, dogs don't derive their courage from their relative the wolf. Another well-known writer on dogs, Vicki Hearne, points out that a wolf "will not have the courage of a good dog, the courage that springs from the dog's commitments to the forms and significance of our domestic virtues."[9]

Here's just a small sampling of Dogs of Courage throughout the centuries:

- In the Swiss Alps, Great Saint Bernard Pass is named for the heroic dogs who rescued hikers who had lost their way or were caught in avalanches.
- As early as the eighteenth century, police learned to train dogs to work alongside them.
- In the 1920s, the aviator Charles Lindbergh developed his flying chops with a dog named Booster sitting shotgun in the passenger seat.
- During World War II, dogs helped patrol the beaches and borders of the United States to keep an eye out for spies and intruders.

Dogs have proved their mettle in recent disasters as well, from helping to recover survivors after the bombing of the Alfred P. Murrah Federal Building in Oklahoma City in 1995 to searching for people left behind in flooded homes in New Orleans in the aftermath of Hurricane Katrina.

And of course dogs played a vital role in New York City in the weeks and months after 9/11, first to search for people in the rubble and then to serve as therapy dogs for workers and volunteers who needed a bright spot in weeks filled with despair.

More courageous dogs throughout history

are explored in each chapter of *Dogs of Courage*.

SENSES: WHERE DOGS EXCEL

One of the reasons that dogs can become Dogs of Courage is because of their highly acute senses of smell and hearing. That, combined with their unique capacity for loyalty, gives most dogs the ideal skill set for doing their jobs.

When it comes to sense of smell, dogs clearly excel. Whereas humans have around forty million olfactory receptors in their noses, dogs have around two billion, which means their sense of smell can be up to one hundred times better, depending on the breed.

"Their sense of smell is so good — for instance, with a cheeseburger, we might only smell the cheese or the burger, but they smell the cheese, the pickle, the tomato, and the lettuce," said U.S. Air Force Staff Sergeant Patrick D. Spivey, a military working dog handler teamed up with Bodro, a Belgian Malinois. "It is almost as if they smell it all in 3-D."[10]

"A dog can actually detect whether a scent is coming to his left nostril or his right," said Louise Wilson, head trainer at Wagtail UK, a company that trains dogs in several areas of detection, from explosives to drugs. "The dog's brain and the dog's nose is amazing — I don't think there is any machine that can rival their senses."[11]

"A K-9 can find what he is looking for in a box of black pepper hidden inside a container of mothballs," says Marilyn Jeffers Walton, author of *Badge on My Collar: A Chronicle of Courageous Canines*.

And they can do it at a distance, too, up to 250 yards away with no distractions and about 50 yards away with wind and lots of competing scents. In fact, one study conducted at the Canine Detection Research Institute at Auburn University in Alabama — which has a department devoted to studying military working dogs — theorizes that dogs have the ability to detect the equivalent of a single drop in an Olympic-size swimming pool, which translates to fewer than five hundred parts per trillion.

"If it has an odor and that odor can be identified, you can teach a dog to locate it," said Jill Marie O'Brien, cofounder of the National Canine Scent Work Association. "The dog's nose is like a machine. Nature has created something that human beings can't duplicate artificially."[12]

"Dogs have the incredible ability to determine the direction that a person has walked because the fact [is] that the odor in the direction walked is always fresher than the odor in older sections of the trail," explains Allen Goldblatt, of the Center for Applied Animal Behavior for Security Purposes at Tel Aviv University. "Dogs are even capable of determining the direction of travel by detecting the concentration gradient when the difference in concentration of the scent at the start of the trail was only two seconds older than the scent at the end of the trail."

And once a dog is hot on a trail, you better get out of the way. "When a dog is searching for an olfactory cue, the amount of sniffing increases, and the more difficult the task, the greater the sniff rate," Goldblatt adds.

In a remarkable example of the power of a dog's nose, Goldblatt tells this story: "In a controlled experiment, the FBI gave a Bloodhound a letter written by a woman who had moved to a new house in a different state 6 months prior to writing the letter. Using the scent from the letter, the dog was able to select the house where she had previously lived even though she had not approached the house for 6 months."[13]

"I tell people they're buying a nose with four legs to carry it," jokes handler José "Pepe" Peruyero of the J&K Canine Academy in High Springs, Florida. "They love to eat, love to smell. It's what they live for."[14]

Lieutenant John Pappas with the New York City Police Department agrees. "The real technology [in police work] is the dog, and a lot of it is centered on the nose," he said. "That's the most useful tool we have."[15]

They're no slouches when it comes to hearing, either, which is at once broader and more selective than humans'. A dog can hear up to 35,000 Hz per second while humans can barely manage 20,000, which means it's a piece of cake for them to hear footsteps nearby even if a fighter jet is taking off right next to them. They're also more sensitive to high-pitched noises and have the ability to close off their inner ear, which can help them block out background sounds in order to concentrate on a noise that's directly in front of them.

It's this combination of natural sensory perfection that makes Dogs of Courage so much better attuned to the world. Sometimes it seems like they're clairvoyant and have a sixth sense that helps them to do their jobs. One bonus is that it also helps the humans around them to save a huge amount of time. "[Dogs] help the investigators try and determine if it was an arson or an accidental fire," said Chief Garry Alderman of Horry County Fire Rescue in South Carolina. "[They have] helped us tremendously as far as pinpointing some arsons throughout the county. The sensitivity of their noses is just unbelievable. If we didn't have a dog, you'd have to go in there with a piece of instrumentation, and it would probably take you five times longer."[16]

Conventional thinking in the scientific community when it comes to a dog's abilities has come a long way. "In the eighties, we thought, Let's build a machine that can mimic the dog!" said Robert Gillette, the director of the Animal-Health and Performance Program in the College of Veterinary Medicine at Auburn University in Alabama. "But you can't mimic a dog. It's just a superior mechanical working system. So in the nineties we began to think, Hmm, let's put some of that research into the animals."[17]

Significantly, training methods have changed as well. "You used to wait until the dog did something wrong, then corrected it," said Michele Pouliot, director of research and development at Guide Dogs for the Blind. "Now you're rewarding a behavior you like before it goes wrong. If you're constantly on top of him — punishing, punishing, punishing — that behavior is not going away. You have to get that dog to try to figure out what you want."[18]

Indeed, the study of dogs is spreading

throughout the culture. It's not just for dog trainers anymore and may go a long way toward helping those who are experts in the study of humans to expand their horizons. "For psychologists, dogs may be the next chimpanzees," said the psychologist Paul Bloom. Bruce Blumberg chose to address this question by offering a course at the Harvard Extension School titled "The Cognitive Dog: Savant or Slacker." It turned out that Blumberg was on to something; the topic was so intriguing that the course quickly turned into the second-largest psychology course offered that semester, though Blumberg came in for a fair bit of criticism for suggesting that dogs could ever be slackers.

"In the last couple of years there have been a number of scientific studies . . . on certain social problems involving humans, [and] dogs seem to be better able to perform the task than chimpanzees," said Blumberg. "For example, using pointing gestures to find hidden food is something the dogs respond to better than chimps. A dog has been shown to learn words really, really quickly based on one or two repetitions, so they are able to associate a novel word with a novel object. This is something never seen in chimps."[19]

Whether they do it full- or part-time, all Dogs of Courage are working dogs, and in many cases they're just doing what they were born to do.

In fact, dogs have always worked. It's been only in the last few decades that humans have thought the best way to treat dogs is to coddle them, serving as a kind of helicopter parent to their canine companion.

Certainly, some breeds do best as companion dogs, particularly the toy breeds. However, the vast majority of dogs — like people — thrive when they have a task to perform that serves a useful purpose. And when they don't, watch out.

"Before the industrial era, dogs spent their days in the company of men doing serious work: hunting, fishing, herding, guarding, and hauling," writes Diana Schaub. "Now imagine today's suburban or apartment dog, utterly without employment or even companionship for most of the day. Children are at least sent to daycare, but dogs are left to their own devices. Is it any wonder they end up as canine delinquents, barking and biting inappropriately?"[20]

Every dog needs a job. Ebony, a black giant schnauzer, is living proof of this credo. Her owners, Mike and Melenda Lanius, own a cleaning service in Pekin, Illinois, including a sideline business called MoldBlasters. They sent Ebony to the Florida Canine Academy for three months to learn how to become a mold-sniffing dog, for two reasons: They wanted to use her services in their business, but more important, they believed that providing the dog with a clear purpose would help to calm her down, since she was hyper and prone to fits of excitement.

Both hunches panned out. Today, both Ebony and her owners are living happier lives. And the Laniuses started yet another business: Top Dog Inspection Services, where Ebony and two other schnauzers work. "Before Ebony went to school, she was hyper and bored," said Melenda Lanius. "She was bouncing off the walls. Now she's a lot calmer. She has a job, and she loves it. Say 'work,' and her ears prick up. She is one working girl who never has a case of the Mondays."[21]

While dogs like Ebony typically work for food or praise after they locate the item they're looking for, some trained dogs don't require rewards since their drive to work is so strong. "For certain types of work, the task serves as the reward," said William S. Helton. "Reinforcers such as food and praise are not needed. Access to the task is all that is needed to reinforce correct behaviors. Denying a dog an opportunity to work is punishment."[22]

"The role of working dogs in society is far greater than most people know and is likely to increase, not diminish, in the future," Helton writes. "Working dogs are unique because of the ease with which they work in complex human settings and integrate into human society."[23]

And just like people, each dog is different in the way he approaches his job. "Every dog has its own unique style, its own unique ability to scent," said Matt Zarrella, a corporal with the Rhode Island State Police. "Some scent dogs are physically better at negotiating obstacles and hanging in there on long, hot days and working through for longer periods of time than others. We think the German shepherd is a great animal. They transition well when trained to perform two or more types of specialties."[24]

At the same time, though dogs may display great enthusiasm for the task at hand, it's important for the people who work with them to realize that again, just like humans, they do have their physical and emotional limits. "Dogs aren't machines, they can't be turned off and placed on the shelf, and they vary as individuals," said Aimee Hurt, cofounder of Working Dogs for Conserva-

BELGIUM

Sometimes Dogs of Courage connect with people because of a commonality. In the case of Belgium, a four-year-old Australian shepherd, that commonality strikes when she meets someone in her line of therapy dog work who is also disabled in some way.

You see, Belgium is blind and partially deaf; her condition is common among a particular type of Aussie known as a lethal white shepherd, which is most often caused by irresponsible breeding. She works as a therapy dog mostly with hospice and cancer patients around Mesa, Arizona.

But it almost didn't happen. Her original owners gave Belgium up when she wasn't getting along with another dog in the household. She was scheduled for euthanasia, but a volunteer at the shelter called the organization Amazing Aussies Lethal White Rescue of Arizona, which took her in and placed her with a foster family that ended up adopting her.

Lauran and Jay Beebe, her new owners, had some work to do, since Belgium hadn't gotten much exercise at her previous home. After about six weeks, Belgium worked up to walking a mile every day and now enjoys her daily walks and even plays nice with the other family dogs.

This by itself would have been enough of a success story, but once Belgium's true colors showed through, the Beebes decided that she might have the kind of temperament suitable for therapy dog work. After an initial assessment and training program, in January 2009 she began visiting local hospitals, long-term care facilities, and hospices once or twice a week.

Due to her own disabilities, she works solely on intuition to provide comfort and relief to both patients and their families, who are often emotionally and physically drained as well. She often visits a paraplegic patient who cannot talk and is able to move only her left hand. When Belgium visits, the dog sits on her bed and the

Photo: Lauran Beebe

woman visibly relaxes as she strokes her coat. Nurses on the floor refer to Belgium's ultrasoft fur as "the healing coat." She also often sits with patients in the infusion room while they receive chemotherapy.

People relate to Belgium because of her disabilities. Many of the patients she visits have lost their eyesight or hearing due to trauma or age, and they readily feel a kinship with the dog, who has to deal with her own challenges. Belgium maneuvers around beds, chairs, and other obstacles in a patient's room with grace — and also the occasional bump on the head.

"Belgium is very responsive to sick and elderly people and really seems to shine at her job," says Lauran Beebe. "She is truly blessed for this job and has made a difference in many people's lives. Belgium will continue to volunteer her time and love as long as she is physically able. Belgium is living proof that disabled does not mean disposable."

tion, a Montana-based group. "They come with unique strengths: They are very mobile, they are able to problem-solve, they are able to learn and adapt."[25]

With that said, it's important to note that

some people — dog lovers and not — don't believe it's wise for dogs to work. Instead, they insist dogs are best served by being spoiled rotten, with three meals a day, some cuddling, a couple of walks, and as much *Animal Planet* as they can stand. Especially in today's society where most people choose a pet primarily for companionship, some dog lovers think it's cruel for a dog to herd sheep, help a police officer do her job, or work in a war zone.

Indeed, even respected animal experts have expressed ambivalence about the issue. While a card-carrying member of People for the Ethical Treatment of Animals would probably think it was heartless or dangerous for a dog to be out herding cattle or heading into an abandoned building to pursue a suspect, Kristin Mehus-Roe said that it wasn't until she had adopted Desi, one of a breed of cattle dog called an Australian kelpie, that she had second thoughts about adopting a dog for the sole purpose of giving it a good home.

After a stranger chided her for keeping Desi as a pet, saying it would "break [the dog's] spirit," Mehus-Roe came to terms with the lecture. "She's had a fine life with a lot of walks and playtime, two annoying little 'sister' dogs, and a lot of people who love her," she wrote in her excellent book *Working Dogs: True Stories of Dogs and Their Handlers*. "I instinctively cringed away from the idea of using a dog as a beast of burden, but is that really what it is? We're shocked by their desire to do the work they were bred for, but if some dogs are unsatisfied with the lives we give them, would a working life be better?"

She then admits the uneasy truth: "Desi has never been particularly happy. She's really only content when we're out doing something. Some dogs are made to work."

Indeed, only then can they receive the opportunity to show that they are truly Dogs of Courage.

Mehus-Roe also points out the tragic effects when dogs born to be heroes don't get the chance: "Millions of dogs are relinquished to animal shelters each year simply because their families don't understand their need to work," she said. "High-energy Border Collies or Jack Russell terriers are abandoned or euthanized because they'd become destructive after being left in a backyard all day. It is tragic when a dog is abandoned simply for doing the job we bred it to do."[26]

Even the Dog Whisperer, Cesar Millan, believes it's better for everyone if a dog has a specific purpose in life. "Animals need to work for food and water," he noted. "The ones that get food and water just because they're cute — those are my clients."[27]

On the brighter side, some dogs are able to show their courageous sides by just being themselves, and can often bring levity and cheer to an environment that sorely needs it.

Like in Washington, D.C., for example. No Border Collies here, but fluffy smaller dogs who help clear the air of tension in a place where stress is second nature. And regardless of the political affiliation of their human counterparts, the dogs' constant presence has helped at least one legislator to reach across the aisle.

Representative Ed Whitfield (R-KY) regularly brings three dogs to his office on Capitol Hill: Julep, a Labrador mix; a Scottish terrier named Bosley; and a Jack Russell terrier named Nigel. He believes that their presence helps bring a sense of humor and sanity to a place that tends to be full of self-importance. "I think the atmosphere is better, because it's hard to be very formal when you have a dog jumping around the office," he said.[28]

THE HUMAN BOND

In the end, even though every canine walking the earth is a potential Dog of Courage — some just haven't had a chance to prove themselves yet — the truth is that it usually takes somebody on the other end of the leash to help bring it out.

Indeed, developing a strong partnership rewards both dog and human many times over throughout their lifetimes, even if that partnership is a short one. Dog lovers are already gratified with the instant smiles that appear on the faces of complete strangers whenever they and their dog walk into a room. But the dogs obviously benefit as well.

"We want to know how the animals are benefiting from the exchange," says Rebecca A. Johnson, who leads the Research Center for Human/Animal Interaction at the University of Missouri College of Veterinary Medicine. She's studied how dog walking has helped humans to become healthier and exercise more — many even boosted their non-dog-walking exercise sessions during the week — but she has also turned the spotlight on how it's helped the dogs.

For instance, most animal shelters and humane organizations encourage volunteers to come in and walk dogs who are up for adoption. "We found that [the dogs] were significantly more likely to be adopted if they were in the dog-walking group," said Johnson. She theorizes that regular visits from friendly humans help make the dogs more socialized and help to even out canine hormones, which can get quite stressed due not only to the shelter environment but also to insufficient exercise.[29]

There's some scientific evidence for this. A 2004 study at the Tshwane University of Technology in Pretoria, South Africa, discovered that after a twenty-minute session together, the good-mood hormones oxytocin, prolactin, and endorphin jumped for dogs and humans. More intriguingly, cortisol levels decreased significantly during the experiment; cortisol is a hormone produced by the body in times of stress.

Dr. Johnson agrees with the study's findings, and particularly zeroed in on the boost in oxytocin levels. "Oxytocin helps us feel happy and trusting," she said. "Oxytocin has some powerful effects for us in the body's ability to be in a state of readiness to heal, and also to grow new cells, so it predisposes us to an environment in our own bodies where we can be healthier."[30]

In the end, the simple truth is that dogs make us feel better and act better, not only for ourselves but for the world at large.

"So long as they remain by our sides," writes Diana Schaub, "we have the possibility, through the canine mirroring of qualities that humans praise or blame, of recovering the heroic sense."[31]

CHAPTER TWO:
POLICE DOGS

Perhaps more so than any other profession-ally trained Dog of Courage, the police dog is a jack-of-all-trades, a Renaissance canine in a sense. Particularly in smaller police departments where there may be only one or two K-9 teams, in the course of a normal working day a police dog may be called upon to perform a search and rescue, scope out a building, sniff out drugs or a possible bomb, track a suspect or a missing person, or help comfort a lost child.

Or just tag along with his human partner on patrol while making a few new friends on the way.

In big city departments, however, dogs tend to fit into one specialty — detection or patrol, say, but not both. And as expected, the stress level is ratcheted up since canine teams are more likely to get called for a crime in progress and encounter the bad guys face-to-face.

Regardless of whether dogs are in a small town or in a city with millions of people, their human partners never take their canine sidekicks for granted. As one policeman put it, "When you do traffic stops, it's a great feeling to know the dog is back there. That dog will save your ass more than you ever know. He will be better than another cop."[1]

"You have helicopters for surveillance and radios and patrol cars and investigators," said Captain Tim Simon, who heads up an Orange County–based regional drug task force. "But there is nothing you can rely on . . . as [much as] a well-trained dog and handler."[2]

Today, there are K-9 units working for municipal police departments, county sheriffs, state troopers, and in a slew of other city, county, state, and federal government departments. While the logistics may vary, there are some commonalities about police dogs:

- Most police dogs live with their handlers.
- Training is ongoing; many handlers spend at least an hour a day in police-specific exercises with their dogs.
- A police dog may look approachable, but for civilians it's a good idea to always ask first before reaching out to pat one on the head.

That last point is particularly important. "These dogs are often the face of the department," said Officer Gary Schad of the Tucson Police Department.[3] Schad was the partner of Miko, a four-year-old German shepherd who died in 2006 while on the job.

Indeed, though they are just as well trained as their human counterparts, canine police dogs could also realistically bear the title of public relations manager. Police officers across the country readily admit that their canine units help build goodwill in the community and also go a long way toward thwarting children who may be thinking about pursuing a future life in crime. After all, police dogs and their handlers often appear at local schools and after-school groups to talk about a life in police work.

In Cottage Grove, Minnesota, Blitz, the first police dog on the force, was in high demand and making public appearances all over town. "It may seem pretty fluffy, like a marketing department for the police, but some of it is of real value," said city administrator Ryan Schroeder. "Children grow up feeling comfortable that police are there to assist them, not just to be some bad guy or gal in blue."[4]

"It's a huge PR thing," said Jeff Gottstein, a police officer and handler in Woodbury,

Minnesota. "It's a feel-good thing."

On the other side of the same coin, Gottstein said that police dogs provide great "psychological deterrence" to the other side; in other words, in the event of a riot or confrontation with a criminal, potential problems are much more likely to be avoided if a trained dog is present. "In the seven years I have been with [a police dog], I haven't had a single physical confrontation," said Gottstein. "Someone might be willing to fight me, but they aren't willing to fight the dog."[5]

There can be no doubt that criminals are well aware of how well police dogs can do their jobs. In fact, drug traffickers have offered up to $30,000 as a bounty to anyone who kills a drug-detection dog. When you consider that back in 1990, Rocky, a Belgian Malinois drug-detection dog, was able to locate a stash of cocaine from Mexico with a street value of $128 million, canine police are worth every bit of kibble paid for with taxpayer dollars.

"They are such an effective tool," Sergeant Rod Mamero of Utah's Payson Police Department said. "Without a dog, we might have to rely on deadly physical force."[6]

Officer Kenny Geib, who works at the Lancaster County Prison in Pennsylvania, agrees. "When a police officer pulls his gun and fires a bullet, he can't bring it back," he said. "We have to demonstrate that we can control and call back our dogs, which are our lethal weapons."[7]

In addition, these dogs are trained to give their lives for their handlers. "[A dog's] fierce and protective loyalty and his ability to control his aggression all combine to make him a perfect partner," said Marilyn Jeffers Walton, author of *Badge on My Collar: A Chronicle of Courageous Canines*. "He is a deterrent to crime, and his presence often means gunshots will not have to be fired."[8]

In addition to K-9 units in police departments, police dogs are used in a variety of other state and federal agencies:

- The Federal Bureau of Investigation trains dogs to detect explosives. Like other canine teams, FBI dogs all live with their handlers; but unlike other canine teams, the FBI uses only Labrador retrievers in their program, as they believe they're calmer and more people-friendly than other breeds. FBI dogs are trained to find up to nineteen thousand different combinations of explosives.
- The U.S. Customs and Border Protection has used dogs as a vital part of

their security forces since 1974. Canine teams work along the border, in airports, and in warehouses to detect everything from drugs and humans to currency and bombs. The agency uses a variety of breeds, from shepherds and Labs to mixed-breed shelter rescues.

- Over at the Department of Agriculture, the Beagle Brigade rules. Their aim: to sniff out contraband produce, meat, and other edibles before they make it into the country. Beagles are used because they have such a high drive for food.

Dogs have served alongside police officers in Europe since the 1700s, mostly Bloodhounds to track escaped convicts and criminals.

Training programs were introduced and became mainstream during both world wars. In fact, Germany had over thirty thousand dogs operating in various military capabilities over the course of World War I; when war first broke out, Germany already had six thousand dogs trained and ready to go, which was no surprise since they had such a huge head start: The German Army founded the first military program specifically to train dogs in 1884, near Berlin.

These programs formed the foundation for training today's police dogs, though formal police programs did not start in earnest in the United States until the 1970s, and they did not become widespread until twenty years later. And their purposes — and training — were very different.

"Up until the 1970s, the police just wanted dogs that would bite everyone," said Jim Matarese, past president of the United States Police Canine Association. "They'd go to the pound and get dogs that were fear biters, just scared to death of people."[9]

Then in the 1980s, demand for drug-sniffing dogs grew as crack cocaine became a nationwide epidemic. Today, departments all over the country recognize the value of a well-trained canine team, and as a result, they're clamoring for them. In fact, since 2001, the number of police officers in New York City has dropped by 17 percent but the number of canine police teams has essentially doubled.

"One canine team can do the work of ten or fifteen guys in a gang situation," said Lieutenant John Pappas of the NYPD. "When you throw in some jaws and paws, it changes the landscape. It's like pulling up in an M1 Abrams battle tank."[10]

In fact, in a study conducted in 2000 by Officer Marie Wolfe of the Lansing, Michigan,

Police Department's K-9 unit, canine teams were successful in locating suspects 93 percent of the time, while teams that contained only humans succeeded 59 percent of the time. The dogs also found each suspect five to ten times faster than the non–K-9 teams.

As dog trainers like to say, emotions and moods travel down the leash; in other words, a dog can easily pick up on the feelings and present mood of his handler and since police are constantly dealing with the unknown and the possibility that a lethal threat could be just around the next corner, it's no surprise that a canine patrol member would be on edge and always alert for anything or anyone who could do harm.

"They're trained for handler protection, and they don't know when that threat is going to be upon them," said Sergeant Randy Brenner of the NYPD.[11]

There's a constant balancing act between a dog and his handler. After all, the dog is out there, nose first, looking for any and all threats; it's the handler's duty to put on the brakes while also letting the dog do his job.

"If it's not a violent felon, you typically don't send in the dog," said Gary Pietropaolo, a retired K-9 police officer who now runs his own dog-training business in upstate New York. "In the use-of-force scale, it's almost equal to using a nightstick."[12]

Having a canine partner cuts down on collateral damage, which often breeds goodwill when searching in areas where people may be hostile to the presence of a police officer. No matter whether a dog is patrolling a neighborhood or searching for explosives, this usually frees up the two-legged officers on the force to do other tasks. In addition, the degree of damage is limited if dogs do a task that would normally be left to humans. For instance, instead of forcing open a car trunk or breaking down a door to check for drugs or a bomb, relying on a dog's superior sense of smell means there are fewer false leads.

Whether they're looking for drugs or bombs, detection dogs all have something in common: They are trained to sit still whenever they locate an item of interest. Then the human counterparts move in and take over to confirm the find. This passive response is in contrast to past canine training methods when a dog either barked or was encouraged to attack and dig to uncover the item. The current technique helps to preserve evidence and prevent explosives from going off.

"A passive response is where a dog sits as still as possible when he finds something," said Crystal Greer, a contract handler working with American K-9 Detection Services, a company that trains dogs for service in the military and with law enforcement agencies. "They get as close as they possibly can to what they think is the source and then they 'respond,' sending messages to the handlers."[13]

THE IDEAL POLICE DOG

What kinds of dogs are best suited for police work? Though dogs of all shapes, sizes, and breeds have served in police departments throughout the country for standard patrol and detection work, the majority of K-9 units favor a male dog between one and two years old. Males are larger than females — and therefore more threatening in instances where that's important — as well as more curious. Plus, male dogs are left unneutered in many cases, which helps them remain aggressive, though that is held in check with proper training.

Shepherds are generally the dog of choice, especially Belgian Malinois and German shepherds. Police work can be long and tedious and require high endurance from both dog and human; often smaller dogs just aren't up to the task. Small dogs also can be more temperamental, a negative trait for dogs that have to get along with the public. Larger dogs, like Great Danes and Dobermans, are also frowned upon: They may be too large to squeeze into a small area, and the life spans of bigger dogs tend to be shorter than medium-sized dogs, an important consideration given the sizable investment of time and money in training them.

For many departments, the ideal dogs come from Europe, especially from breeders in Germany and Slovakia. They may be more expensive, but the benefits are many. European breeders are required to follow more stringent standards. But perhaps more important, dogs bred for police work are sent to canine police academies before they even cross the pond. And so aside from some cultural differences, a European-trained police dog will arrive at an American police department ready to hit the ground running; the only issue is that his human coworkers may have to learn a bit of German or Slovak in order to give the dog commands. However, many police officers say it's worth it because most suspects won't know that the dog is about to attack.

The federal government lays out specific requirements for dogs used in the Department of Homeland Security as well as U.S. Customs and Border Protection, which runs two separate canine training facilities: the Canine Enforcement Training Center in Front Royal,

Virginia, and the National Canine Facility in El Paso, Texas.

Here are the specifications:

- Breed: A recognized working or sporting breed, such as Labrador retriever, golden retriever, German shepherd, Dutch shepherd, or Belgian Malinois.
- Lineage: European-born or of European lineage traceable for two generations. American-bred canines may be accepted as determined by the government.
- Age: Between twelve and thirty-eight months.
- Weight: No less than forty-five pounds or more than ninety pounds.
- Size: No less than twenty-two inches or more than thirty inches at the shoulder.

Of course, this is just the beginning. He may have the bones and breeding, but when it comes to behavior, a potential police dog has to prove himself. After all, he has to react differently from other Dogs of Courage. For instance, while therapy dogs need to allow small children to pull their ears and yank their tail without barking or snarling, police dogs have to react by growling or barking, or by merely giving a nasty look in the direction of a perpetrator.

At the same time, a good police dog must share certain characteristics with a guide or service dog. Being easily distracted is a negative, since the ability to ignore other dogs and strangers who want to pet the nice doggy is paramount. A well-trained police dog should respond only to his handler and not shy away in the presence of loud and sudden noises, like gunfire and yelling.

TRAINING — DOGS AND HUMANS

The human half of a canine team can't just jump in and start driving around with a dog in the backseat of a police cruiser. Both partners must first prove their worth.

First, the humans: To be considered for a canine team, they must pay their dues. Most police departments require that officers put in at least three or four years on the regular force before moving on to the canine department. Their track record must be stellar, with numerous arrests and convictions and no demerits or bad marks during their tenure. And since canine teams also serve in a public relations capacity, introverts need not apply.

Most important, however, future canine officers must be in good physical shape.

MIDGE

The Guinness Book of World Records has long included record-breaking dogs, like the one with the longest tongue — claimed by a Pekinese named Puggy whose tongue measures a full four and a half inches — and Hercules, an English mastiff who held the title of largest living dog in January 2012, at 282 pounds.

But the title of the smallest police dog in the world falls to an eight-pound Chihuahua–rat terrier mix named Midge who makes her home in Geauga County, Ohio, with her partner, Sheriff Dan McClelland. Midge joined the K-9 unit of the Geauga County Sheriff's Office when she was only ten weeks old — and weighed in at just above two pounds.

Sheriff McClelland had been looking for a canine assistant to help him cover the county east of Cleveland, with a population of around ninety thousand people.

Photo: Daniel C. McClelland, Geauga County Sheriff

The purpose of the dog: to help find drugs, which were becoming a larger problem in the area.

The department had always had larger dogs as part of their K-9 team, but McClelland became intrigued by the idea of bringing a smaller dog on staff when he learned that some people were suing police departments across the country after larger K-9 staff — like German shepherds and Labs — had damaged personal property in the pursuit of drugs on a police call. "Plus, a 100-pound German shepherd fills up a car's interior or trunk," said McClelland. "It's awkward and hard for a dog this size to move."*

Fate intervened when a coworker's Chihuahua had puppies. The father was a rat terrier — a breed of dog intent on finding its prey — and when the coworker said there was one puppy left, the runt of the litter, McClelland knew he had to take a look.

When they were formally introduced, he knew she would make a good drug-detection dog. "She was very calm around people," he said. "All kinds of strange folks pass through a sheriff's office, so being comfortable and confident would definitely be a plus. Second, I noticed that she sniffed everything." Though the dog was a tiny puppy, McClelland took it as a sign. "She [already] understood what her nose was for."[†]

He took her home, named her Midge after Barbie's sidekick, and started training her almost immediately. She aced her state certification test and started being credited with drug finds on a regular basis. Once word got out about the tiny narcotics-detection dog, everyone wanted to meet her. Midge has appeared on the *Rachael Ray Show, Fox and Friends,* CNN, and MSNBC, among others. In addition to her drug sniffing, an important part of Midge's job is community relations.

McClelland often brings Midge to schools to talk to kids about drugs, as well as to the county jail. No matter where they go, she always makes people smile, especially when she dons her special biker goggles and goes for a ride with McClelland on the department motorcycle.

"I tell the kids, 'Even when you're small, if you take a stand you can make a difference,'" said the sheriff.[‡]

---

[*]Anderson and Anderson, *Angel Dogs with a Mission,* pp. 46–47.
[†]Ibid., pp. 47–48.
[‡]Connie Mabin, "Small Dog Has Big Nose for Sniffing Out Crime," *Cincinnati Post,* July 31, 2006.

After all, working side by side with a canine partner requires stamina, as well as virtually daily training. In addition, the hours can be long; with active duty, paperwork, and training sessions, a canine team can be on the job as much as sixty hours a week. "They have to have a stable home environment, maturity, be physically fit and [have] an ability to multitask," said Sergeant Derrick Hesselein of the Alameda County Sheriff's Office in Northern California.[14]

Advanced screening is necessary; the department wants to make sure that canine officers will stick with it for a dog's entire career. Once a human and canine police team bond, there's usually no backing out: Police dogs and officers are matched for life.

After the humans jump through all the hoops, the dogs must pass muster. While some police departments prefer to purchase their dogs already trained and then tweak them according to the specific needs of their department, some would rather acquire dogs before they've gone through extensive training. Only then can they train the dog to their own specifications and needs. "We want a dog we can take into the schools," said Lieutenant Michael Phelps, department head for the Mission Police Department's K-9 division in McAllen, Texas.[15]

Finally, it's time to match human and dog. "We want the dog to make up for where the handler is weak and vice versa," said Sergeant Randy Brenner. "But I'll tell you, after a while the person's personality becomes similar to the dog's."[16] And sometimes, the department screens the dogs to make sure they're a good fit with the human officers currently on staff.

"We tested about 20 dogs to get the five we liked best," said Sergeant Hesselein. "We wanted to match the dog with the handler. We try to find a nice, healthy balance between the handler and the dog."[17]

As to training, whether it's done in Slovakia or in New York City, some things are similar. First comes basic training, then agility, followed by more specialized training like bomb- or drug-detection skills. Basic training is essentially obedience school, where dogs are taught to sit, heel, and lie down. In addition to spoken commands, police dogs are trained to respond to hand signals, since the handler may be far away or silence may be essential when on a stakeout.

Agility training is also important, since police dogs may be required to climb a ladder or jump through an open window, as well as crawl through a dark, narrow tunnel. Like their human counterparts, police dogs must be physically fit. "A [police] dog must continually be able to go up flights of stairs, over concrete barriers, and in and out of cars," said Jason Bergeron, a contract handler with Canine Associates International.[18]

Search and tracking skills are also important. Whether they will be looking for people or for illegal substances, like drugs, explosives, or even guns, most police dogs are trained in these elementary skills, even if they do not go on to become specially trained detection dogs.

In years past, police dogs were trained to attack without a command from their partners, but those days are long over. When subduing a suspect, police dogs today learn to bark and bite only upon hearing a command from their handler.

One last component of basic police dog training before they are sent off into specialty training is to desensitize dogs to loud noises and explosions. From fireworks to gunfire, these loud, short sudden noises are part of a police officer and police dog's life.

Once a dog becomes a bona fide canine member of the police force, training never ends. "It's not like my dog found marijuana and now I'm done for the day," said Air Force Staff Sergeant Glenn Gordon, who works alongside Ricky, his German shepherd partner. "I also have to maintain the dog's training. He's just like a little kid. If he doesn't continue to tie his shoes, he's going to forget."[19]

Plus there is ample opportunity for canine teams to prove their mettle in competitions and field trials held across the country.

"Anybody can take a dog and say, 'This is a police dog,' but according to whose standards?" says Karen Price, who occasionally judges competitions held by the United Police and Corrections K-9 Association. "We want to see the ability of both the dog and the handler to perform their jobs as a team. And they are a team. The dog is working for the handler, and the handler is working for the dog."[20]

And another thing about being the human half of a canine team: The paperwork will kill you.

"A lot of people don't realize how much paperwork is involved with a dog," said Glenn Gordon. "My dog has been in the military for five years. Every single day of this dog's life, his records have to be updated."[21] After all, when a dog does his job, everything is noted on his permanent record, from weight to training to mood and temperament out in the field to where the dog traveled. Anything that a dog does — like attack — or finds —

like drugs — has to be documented or the case may be thrown out in court.

Technology is starting to catch up with canines' natural talents. Some police departments are investing in special infrared cameras that are mounted on the dogs' backs. They come with tiny wireless microphones and doggy earbuds so that a handler can give commands while listening to sounds from the dog's vantage point. "We can see what the dog is seeing," says Lieutenant John Pappas. "We can use it in a building search. If there's a suspicious box, instead of sending a human being down there, I'll send in the dog, then call him back if things look suspicious."[22]

LEAVING THE FORCE

A typical police dog's career lasts only six or seven years. Canine senses start to fade and become less sharp around age ten. Unlike military police dogs, who typically spend only two years with a handler before being rotated on to another one, police dogs tend to spend their entire careers with just one handler, living at home with him and his family, acting like any regular family pet, relaxing and socializing with friends and family. In virtually all cases, when a police dog is retired, he lives out his golden years with

ZEUS

There are tens of thousands of police dogs all across the country who do their jobs and do them well.

There also are a few highly trained elite canines who go above and beyond the call of duty and make it difficult for others not to sit up and take notice.

Zeus, a German shepherd with the New York City Police Department, was the most highly decorated dog in the department's history. And like Forrest Gump, he was at most of the major historical events that took place during his life.

Zeus and Officer Robert Schnelle were paired up when the dog was only eight weeks old. Zeus became the first certified search-and-rescue dog in the department and hit the ground running, working on several high-profile cases, including the first bombing of the World Trade Center in 1993.

Zeus and Schnelle also helped out whenever FEMA needed reinforcements in the wake of natural and urban disasters. They traveled to Oklahoma City to help out after the bombing of the Murrah Federal Building in 1995; Zeus found twenty-four victims of the blast and was entered in the Oklahoma Pet Hall of Fame as a result of his work. A few months after returning from Oklahoma City, Zeus helped to solve an eight-year-old open murder case by finding the body of a man that had been wrapped in plastic and buried under four feet of concrete.

"When Zeus was digging, he was on a mission. He was a great dog, a happy dog, a sociable dog," said Schnelle. "He was one in a million."*

The following year he headed to Atlanta to help find clues to the bombing at the 1996 Olympics and also visited a few Caribbean islands to perform search-and-rescue operations in the wake of several hurricanes.

Oh, and when he was at home, Zeus was no slouch: He also helped patrol the streets with his human partner.

Zeus left the force to live out a well-deserved retirement at Officer Schnelle's North Bellmore, Long Island, home in 2000. Though Schnelle continued to work as a K-9 team with his new partner, Atlas, the whole family obviously had a soft spot for his longtime partner.

When Zeus died on July 23, 2002, at the age of ten, all of the Schnelles were devastated, even Atlas, the rookie canine. "They were like father and son," said Schnelle.†

"It's a tough loss. He was a good partner," he added. "My whole family is having a hard time. He was one of us."[‡]

*Stacy Horn, "Zeus — A Cadaver Dog," The RestlessSleep.com, August 19, 2005.
†Phillip Messing, "New York's Furriest Dies at 10," *New York Post,* July 25, 2002.
‡Michele McPhee, "A Hero Police Dog Dies," *New York Daily News,* July 25, 2002.

his handler.

Once it's time for a veteran canine officer to leave the force, it can be difficult for both members of the team to adjust. Jeff Gottstein told of the day he left his freshly retired dog Andy at home and his new canine partner got into his car. "As I left my house, I saw Andy sitting in the window, crying," said Gottstein.[23]

Dogs are sometimes retired before they've had a chance to prove their mettle, because even after ample screening and training, it becomes clear that a particular police dog just isn't the best fit for the job.

In Northumberland in the U.K., Sergeant John Sim of the local police department worked with a shepherd named Vegas, who showed promise but in the end just wasn't cut out to perform all parts of the job.

"She was a bit hesitant and tentative, and

she didn't particularly take to biting," he said. "Although it's not the be-all and end-all of a police dog, it's one of the things that they do have to do. I think it's perhaps because of her more timid nature. Plus, she doesn't particularly like noisy environments with lots of children and she's got a thing about other dogs."

The only option was to find Vegas a new home. "She's actually a lovely, laid-back dog, and for the right people in the right environment, she would make a lovely pet," he said.[24]

Chapter Three:
Fire Dogs

Think of a Dog of Courage who works as a fire dog and the image of a dalmatian, the black-spotted, short-haired dog stereotypically found in firehouses across the country, probably comes to mind.

While this pairing was the case in an era of low-tech firefighting methods, today's fire dogs are more inclined to work in detection mode, sniffing out clues to point arson investigators on the path to finding the cause of a suspicious fire or blaze.

Of course, fire departments still serve as home to more than their fair share of resident dogs — from dalmatians to other breeds and mutts — but today they're more inclined to serve in a companionship capacity than in a professional one.

History

In Great Britain in the eighteenth century, dalmatians were quite the status symbol.

They were the most popular breed to accompany the horse-drawn coaches and carriages of the upper class because of their natural affinity with horses. Dalmatians actually built their firefighting reputation working alongside firefighters and helping to calm the horses, who could prove skittish in the chaos of rushing to a fire as well as at the scene itself. While the firefighters were off trying to extinguish the blaze, the dalmatians would protect not only the horses but also the carriage and equipment from thieves.

On occasion, when it was feared there were people still inside a burning building, with one command from the captain a dog would race into the building, staying low to the ground, and locate any victims. If necessary, these dogs could also climb ladders and crawl through windows before pulling people to safety.

And in cases when it took longer than expected for a firefighter to make his way out of a burning home, a dalmatian was well prepared to enter the building, find a disoriented colleague, and lead him back out to fresh air, in many cases saving his life.

Today, many of the dogs who take up residence in a firehouse have found their way there through a variety of circumstances.

Given the long shifts, sometimes a firefighter brings his dog to work, then the others take such a shine to the canine that he eventually starts to live there full-time. Other dogs are former strays or were given to the firehouse by neighbors, and in a few cases, they've been rescued from fires and accidents where the engine company was called to the scene and then stayed with their saviors.

And though most are no longer trained to run down the stairs and jump inside the cab of a fire engine the instant the alarm goes off, they are no less valuable. In fact, for firehouses located in rough neighborhoods, today's firehouse dog — dalmatian or not — can show his stuff by guarding the premises while his human partners are off battling a blaze.

ARSON-DETECTION DOGS

Today the vast majority of fire dogs work to help detect arson. Known as arson-detection or accelerant-detection dogs, these Dogs of Courage help detectives to pinpoint not only the site of the initial flame but also the type of accelerant used, whether kerosene, gasoline, or lighter fluid.

Like other kinds of detection dogs, their acute sense of smell is so powerful that even though tens of thousands of gallons of water may have been used to extinguish a fire and temperatures may have reached more than 1,000 degrees, incinerating almost everything in its path, specially trained arson dogs will still be able to pick up the scent. They can also alert on scents that are less than fresh. It's not unusual for dogs to alert on a site or specific accelerant that's a couple of months old.

According to insurance industry studies, arson causes approximately 25 percent of the fires reported in the United States each year. After fires caused by cigarettes and other smoking materials, it's the second most common cause of fatalities in house fires.

Arson-detection dogs started to gain traction in the mid-1980s. Mattie was a black Lab attending school at the Guide Dog Foundation, but in 1986 when she was partway through her training, teachers thought she'd make a better detection dog. At the same time, the Connecticut State Police wanted a dog they could specifically train to detect accelerants, since arson was becoming a growing problem. Mattie became the first accelerant-detection dog in the United States. From there, other fire and police departments across the country began to acquire their own arson dogs.

Before dogs, the methods used to detect

the cause of fires were primitive and time-consuming. Investigators used specialized chemical-detection meters to survey a fire scene, take samples, map out each location, and then wait for a lab to come back with results. This often took weeks or even months, and given their rudimentary technology, crucial evidence was often missed altogether.

Having properly trained dogs on the investigation team not only cut way down on the time the process took, but their noses were able to pinpoint the exact spot where an accelerant was placed as well as tell investigators the type of substance used.

"The purpose of having an arson dog on a team is that they're able to, in a matter of an hour or less, go in and identify areas of potential accelerants that it would take days, weeks, sometimes even longer for a human to do," said Heather Paul, a spokeswoman with State Farm Insurance, which actively funds training programs for arson-detection dogs across the country. "The other thing that oftentimes we see is when there is the presence or knowledge that there is an arson dog in an area or on a team, that in and of itself becomes a deterrent for arson."[1]

Steve Gallagher, assistant fire chief in Chillicothe, Ohio, can attest to the time-saving benefits of his trained dog Winchester, a chocolate Lab. "I can spend eight to ten hours digging out a fire scene and not get what I need," he said. "Or I can put my dog out there for 15 minutes. He's a huge time-saver."[2]

"The dog extends the capabilities of the investigator," said Randy Villines, assistant fire chief in Springfield, Missouri. "The scent-discriminating abilities of a canine are better than any equipment we can take to a fire scene when arson is suspected. The canine will lead the investigator to the location of the accelerant, so the investigator can collect an evidence sample and submit [it] to the state's crime labs in order to substantiate the crime of arson."[3]

Sergeant Jeff D. Hamilton has clearly come to appreciate the contributions of his detection dog, a German shepherd named Bizi, to the Horry County Police Department in South Carolina. "Though it's a lot more work than I thought it would be, she really has expanded the capabilities of the department," he said. At the same time, he's learned a few things from her. "[She] always looks so relaxed. I've learned the more relaxed you are, the more the dog relaxes and the better you work."[4]

Many arson investigators and insurance companies believe that Labrador retrievers are the best dogs for arson work. State Farm uses Labs exclusively, for several reasons. Labs are better suited than other dogs to pick out specific odors and to communicate with their handler. Also, their temperament doesn't hurt; they love to work, and the public doesn't generally consider the breed to be threatening, as some might consider a German shepherd. Plus, they love people, which helps when working in a crime scene with many different individuals milling around. They also make great family dogs, which is important since the dogs live with handlers and their families.

Dolph, a black Lab who worked alongside Chief Fire Investigator Bernard W. "Bill" Hardwicke for most of the 1990s out of Los Gatos, California, was a perfect example of why Labs excel as arson dogs. The dog could discern a flammable liquid down to one part per trillion and could pick up on less than a drop of accelerant in still smoldering ashes. Most important, however, arson teams are often called out at night; it wasn't unusual for Dolph and Hardwicke to receive a call at two in the morning and head out the door fifteen minutes later. Some other breeds might change their personalities at night, perhaps becoming more alert — and hostile — to strangers, but Labs tend to tune out such distractions and just focus on the task at hand.

At the time, Dolph was one of only forty-two accelerant-detection dogs in the United States, and because Hardwicke and Dolph were certified on both the state and local level, the ATF called them out for investigations all over the country; as a result, Dolph was the busiest arson dog in the nation. They retired as a team in 2000 — Dolph had six years on the job and Hardwicke had forty-six — after investigating more than thirteen hundred fires throughout the country.

TRAINING

State Farm started its Arson Dog Program in 1993 in response to an increasing number of fires of suspicious origin that resulted in hundreds of deaths and billions of dollars in property loss in the United States each year. The insurance giant recruits handlers from throughout the country, primarily from local and state police agencies as well as fire departments, and pays for their training. In exchange, handlers are required to commit five years to the project and be on call to respond to any investigations in their region, as well as invest the time in continued training to become recertified each year.

Since the launch, more than 250 teams from all over the United States have successfully completed the program and become certified, as well as teams from Canada.

But it's not an easy haul. After a prospective handler is screened and selected — requirements include being able to easily walk three or four miles daily as well as to "walk backward bent over in order to throw targets" — he travels to Maine Specialty Dogs in Gray, Maine, which specializes in training dogs and handlers to become arson investigators. Teams spend eight hours a day for five weeks in intense training, a combination of book learning, agility work, crime scene investigation, and teaching the dog to pick out and indicate a number of different accelerants.

It's not cheap. State Farm estimates that they spend about $23,000 to train each team, which includes costs incurred during the training sessions but also the fee for the dog, since many of the canines come from breeders and guide dog associations, though some come from humane societies and shelters. Unlike other dog and handler arson teams, in the State Farm program, dogs and handlers meet for the first time during training. Plus, State Farm pays about $1,000 each year to help cover training, food, and vet bills for each new recruit.

Before a fire department is approved to

receive a highly trained dog — and thus justify the investment in training the canine as well as his future human handler — State Farm judges the need in a particular city or region. The fire department has to prove that arson is a real problem in their area, with the percentage of unsolved and unprosecuted arson cases well above the national average, and that having a dog available for investigations would help reduce the number of claims paid out for potentially suspicious fires. In its application to the program, the St. Joseph Fire Department in Missouri — which covers an area of seventy square miles with approximately eighty-five thousand people in its jurisdiction — explained that in the ten years from 2002 to 2011, firefighters were called out to 1,590 structure fires, 205 of them due to arson. However, after completing investigations for each, they were able to prosecute only four cases, well below the national average.

In the fall of 2011, a Labrador retriever named Phoenix arrived at the department ready to work after spending five weeks in Maine training with his new handler, Fire Inspector Jason Ziph. Phoenix responded to three structure fires in his first few days on the job. At one, Phoenix detected an accelerant, so his coworkers collected far fewer samples than they would otherwise have had to gather. Ziph already appreciates the efficiency and amount of time and money that Phoenix has saved for the department.

"Instead of 20 or 30 cans of samples, we can send two or three, which means greater efficiency for every agency," he said. "It's working out as a benefit to everyone."[5]

Of course, State Farm is not the only source for highly trained arson dogs. The federal Bureau of Alcohol, Tobacco, Firearms and Explosives relies on skilled detection canines, which they have been training since 1986. Like State Farm, the ATF works with police and fire departments from across the country and provides individual police officers and fire personnel with dogs during a five-week training session at the ATF Canine Training Center in Front Royal, Virginia. The ATF-trained, certified teams then become part of an Accelerant Detection Canine Program, where they make themselves available to the ATF whenever a suspicious fire in their area needs a trained arson dog.

ON THE JOB

Arson dogs are always on call: They live with their handlers, and they never know when they're going to get called out for an investigation.

HOOPER

Though most firehouse dogs these days serve more as mascots than active fire-fighters, Hooper, a dalmatian with Engine Company 211 and Ladder Company 119 in Williamsburg, Brooklyn, was a clear exception.

He was the main canine face of the fire education program in New York City, in ad-

Photo: Richard Hutchings / Digital Light Source

dition to his regular firehouse duties of boosting morale, napping in the dorm, and patiently waiting in the kitchen for stray morsels the cooks would fling his way.

Hooper, born in 1990, had a neat trick that quickly garnered the attention of the thousands of schoolchildren who met him each year as he regularly accompanied Firefighter Kevin Hannafin on hundreds of school visits throughout the region. It was on one particular school visit, however, that he made his mark and cemented his reputation as a celebrity and public figure.

A group of schoolchildren watched transfixed one morning as one of the houses across the street from the school burned. Firefighters were on the scene, but the house was burning so badly that it was too dangerous for them to enter. Suddenly, a man ran out of the house; he was fully engulfed in flames. Though paramedics and firefighters immediately extinguished the flames, the man died. The kids who witnessed this were traumatized, and many had trouble sleeping and eating.

When Hannafin heard the story, he decided that Hooper could help. They visited the class, and he told the kids that Hooper was going to teach them what to do in case they were ever caught in a fire.

Upon Hannafin's command, Hooper stood up and started to walk. Suddenly, he stopped, dropped to the floor, and rolled around, demonstrating the Stop, Drop, and Roll exercise that's standard procedure in firefighting practice.

"When he was one year old, I taught him how to stop, drop, and roll," said Hannafin. "If your clothes or hair should catch on fire, you don't want to run, you want to stop, drop on the ground, cover your face, and roll back and forth to cover the flames."*

Word spread, and Hooper's fame grew well beyond New York City. He appeared on several national TV shows, including the *David Letterman Show,* and in 1995 he won the prestigious Isaac Liberman Service Award, given to a New York City civil service employee who has proved that he's gone above and beyond his job description.

Hooper even had a book written about him. *Firehouse Dog* is a picture book for children that shows a day in the life of the famous dog. New York's mayor at the time, Rudolph Giuliani, even read the book aloud to children when he visited local schools, and sometimes Hooper made a special appearance. The book has sold more than four hundred thousand copies.

Hooper diligently performed his job until

1997, when he started to slow down. He moved from the firehouse to Hannafin's house at the age of nine, where he lived in comfortable retirement until 2002, when he died at the age of twelve.

*Alice McQuillan, "Fire-Safety Dog Hooper Dead," *New York Daily News*, August 21, 2002.

Most arson dogs are food-trained — the only time they eat is after they successfully locate an accelerant. "When a dog sits and indicates an accelerant has been detected, the dog is fed by hand as a reward," said Heather Paul. "If the dog isn't working a fire scene, he or she is trained several times a day for their feeding."[6]

In a dog's own words, courtesy of State Farm: "What that means is even on days when we're not going to fire scenes, several times a day [my handler] Sam places drops of gas around the fire station or his house and says, 'Let's go to work!' As soon as he straps on the food pouch and I hear those words, I'm ready. Whenever I sniff out an accelerant, I sit and point to it with my nose. Sam rewards me with a handful of dog food.

"We do this every day. I always eat at least four cups of food a day; I just never know when I'm going to get it. That helps keep me motivated to work."[7]

Accelerant-detection dogs do share some commonalities with explosive- and drug-detection police dogs, but there are also some important differences.

First, the similarities: It's tough work. Retired fire investigator Susan De Antonio of the Rancho Cucamonga Fire District worked with her accelerant-detection canine Gator for nine years. "Gator's job performance was exemplary, and above expectation in every regard," she said. "He worked in high heat conditions, on broken glass, around dead bodies, and never quit. He always did what I asked of him. He protected my car, my valuables and my personal safety without fail for the entire nine years he was in the field. I never had to worry about my belongings or safety when I was out late on fire lane patrols or bar checks."[8]

Fire dogs often serve as the face of the local firehouse in the eyes of the community members, and a friendly, inviting one at that. And so like their canine police counterparts, fire dogs are often called to make appearances at schools and other public facilities.

In fact, State Farm makes this a requirement for all dog and handler teams that successfully complete their program. The teams give talks and presentations to schools and scout troops about fire safety and the dangers of playing with matches, and they've been known to show up at the public library to help out with story hour. To make sure the kids are paying attention, firefighters often turn the presentation into a show starring the dog by dressing him up or teaching him special tricks that he can perform in front of an appreciative audience.

Of course, there are more ceremonial occasions, like marching in parades, appearing at local fairs and festivals, or just greeting visitors to the firehouse at regular open houses. Regardless of a fire dog's extracurricular activities, the message is the same: "It's amazing with all the technology available, the very best way to fight arson is with a Labrador retriever," says Todd Baker, agency field executive for State Farm.[9]

RETIREMENT

Just like police dogs, there comes a time when an arson dog needs to retire. Though an arson dog's job may not be as difficult or dangerous as a police dog's, age affects a trained arson dog's skills sooner, usually between the ages of nine and ten.

Sometimes a dog leaves the department because her handler retires first, though more than a few human investigators have stayed on the force longer than necessary because the dog still had a few good years of detection work left. And sometimes a combination of a handler's pending retirement and a city's budget woes align so that a fire department will have to go without the most effective means of arson detection around. Or there may not be anyone around with the time, training, or inclination to pick up the mantle.

When fire investigator Susan De Antonio retired from the Rancho Cucamonga Fire District in mid-2009, the Canine Accelerant Detection Program essentially went out of business. Her black Lab Gator had retired two years earlier but helped train Denali, his replacement who was already on the job. The reason the program was suspended was that De Antonio had spearheaded the canine-detection team, launching it in 1994 with her first accelerant-detection dog, a Lab named Newbie, and there was no one else to take up the slack.

In addition, though the department paid for training the dogs, De Antonio covered food, vet bills, and other expenses, which would have been a hard sell to the municipal administration despite the dogs' impressive track records: Denali and Gator investigated more than 140 fires in the region, and one of Gator's major accomplishments involved "testifying" in court by demonstrating his skills in a $1.3 million church arson case, where the arsonist was convicted and given a seven-year prison term.

"We never could have sustained the program had Susan not been a part of it," said Deputy Fire Chief Mike Bell. "She really went above and beyond. I wouldn't say we wouldn't have the program again, but it's highly unlikely."[10]

And like some people, occasionally an arson dog retires just because it's time. Maxine worked alongside her handler Dave Haley for eleven years investigating four hundred to five hundred fires for the Orlando Fire Department.

"Out of hundreds and hundreds of samples I have taken, less than 20 have come back negative," said Haley. "She's 98 percent [accurate]. It's amazing how good that dog is," he added, noting that before Maxine was brought on board, the accuracy rate for human investigators maybe hit 40 percent.[11]

Regardless of the reason for retirement, there's one thing all canine retirees have to learn: to eat out of a food bowl and not out of their handler's hand as a reward for sniffing out an accelerant.

CHAPTER FOUR:
SEARCH-AND-RESCUE DOGS

It's every parent's worst nightmare: a child lost in the woods or buried under rubble.

Twelve-year-old Michael Auberry was camping with his Boy Scout troop in the mountainous part of North Carolina in the late winter of 2007 when he wandered off by himself and couldn't find his way back. Search parties were sent out to look for the boy for four days, with no success. Then they brought in a couple of canine search-and-rescue teams, and the search soon ended when a two-year-old Shiloh shepherd named Gandalf tracked the boy to within a mile of where the scouts had set up their campsite.

After being treated for dehydration and exposure, Michael explained that he had tried to locate the nearest road and flag down a driver to take him home. He had heard the helicopters and people calling for him during his ordeal, but they didn't hear him call back.

Fast-forward almost three years to the devastating aftermath of a magnitude 7 earthquake that hit Haiti. Thousands of people headed to the country to offer what help they could, including highly trained dog-and-handler teams. Though the shoddy infrastructure of the vast majority of homes and buildings in this poverty-stricken nation resulted in thousands of deaths in the capital of Port-au-Prince, rescuers held out hope that they'd be able to save at least a few lives.

Bill Monahan and his Border Collie, Hunter, assigned to California Task Force 2 from the Los Angeles County Fire Department, were among the first rescuers to arrive. They immediately got to work searching through mounds of rubble near the presidential palace, concentrating their search to what were once schools, churches, and apartment buildings.

Rescuers were focused on what used to be a building four stories high when Hunter started to bark, his way of telling Monahan that there was someone alive under all that rock and debris. The dog pinpointed a specific area, and Bill called out. Sure enough, a girl — weakened but joyously still alive — called back, and the other members of the team zeroed in on the spot, first shoring up the rubble and then pulling three girls in all to safety.

"It would have been a reward to find one person alive," said Monahan. "Finding multiple survivors is a huge victory for everyone on the Task Force. It's a giant team effort. From the canines, to the logistics team, to communications, everyone is working at full capacity, using everything we've been trained to do to find survivors. It's an honor to be here."[1]

After they secured the girls' safety, one of Monahan's team members called Wilma Melville, the founder of the Search Dog Foundation back in Ojai, California. "This moment is what SDF Search Teams train for — week in and week out — throughout their careers together," said Melville. "When one SDF team succeeds, *all* of our teams succeed. Their perseverance, skill, and strength in the face of extreme challenges make us all proud, and give us hope."[2]

One a large wilderness area; the other a dangerous confined space amid the chaos and commotion of a disaster area. Still, the method that ultimately found the children was the same: a specially trained search-and-rescue dog.

These Dogs of Courage typically are high energy and extremely motivated by the promise of a ball or toy when the search is complete. Search-and-rescue dogs — also known as SAR dogs — work in a variety of environments and conditions: They are trained to scour hundreds of square miles of vast wilderness where few humans venture or to pinpoint the exact location of a victim buried beneath hundreds of tons of rubble that was once a towering skyscraper in a densely populated area. Some are even trained to work in water or snow and to communicate to a handler whether the subject of their search is alive or not.

And even though SAR handlers accompany their canine partners in a wide variety of environments, they all have one vital thing in common: They absolutely adore the work.

"We are all-volunteer and train for hundreds of hours a year just to make a difference [to] a family that has lost a loved one," said Marie Peck, founder of the Fetch Foundation, a group in Scottsdale, Arizona, that offers a variety of programs that revolve around SAR. She regularly evaluates dogs that have been given up to rescues because they were too hyper to serve as good house pets, which makes them perfect search-and-rescue dogs. "We in the SAR community love that drive," she said.[3] Once the dogs pass their evaluations, which among other skills include stamina and the ability to focus intently de-

Dogs are great searchers," said Dave Mc-Connell, a ski patrol director in Lake Tahoe who worked alongside his golden retriever Kiva, a trained avalanche dog. "If I were in a slide, I'd want them there looking for me. A dog can search a slide area in 30 minutes that would take a team of 10 good probers six to eight hours to cover. A dog can mean the difference between life and death. I've seen Kiva find someone in a drill in three minutes."*

Doc, one of Kiva's peers, is a golden retriever owned and trained by Dave Paradysz, who ran the avalanche dog program at Kirkwood Ski Resort and who ultimately saved the life of twenty-five-year-old Jeff Eckland in January 1993. Eckland was finishing up his night-shift job driving a grooming machine when he was suddenly caught in the path of an avalanche. "The whole mountain gave way," he remembered. "The sound was quite a roar."†

Fortunately, his coworkers had witnessed the massive slide and alerted the ski patrol. Paradysz and Doc were in the vicinity, so as soon as they heard the news, they headed toward the avalanche.

Since Eckland was well versed in avalanche protocol, he knew what to do. "I was just trying to be as calm as possible," he said. "I said to myself, 'you are buried but at least you're in a resort and you're with experienced people.' I kept trying to slow down my breathing to protect whatever oxygen I did have. For the first eight or nine minutes, I was really good at keeping a calm head."

He was also in incredible pain and obviously disoriented. "I assumed I had a big old gnarly juniper branch going through me," he said. "It turns out the avalanche had folded my body in half backward. My heels were right by my face but I didn't know it."

Soon, his calmness disintegrated and he started to panic, which used up what little oxygen remained in the air pocket. "It was starting to get harder to breathe. The last three minutes, I was almost panting like a dog trying to get air. Then I thought, 'I'm dying.' At that point, I started getting tunnel vision. The tunnel slowly started to close, and I was panting and panting and no air was coming. I thought I was history. The tunnel almost closed, and right then Doc's paw broke through and hit my back. I had this incredible inrush of oxygen and could breathe again. I knew it was Doc, and I started screaming, 'Doc! Doc!' It was great."[‡]

In all, Eckland was buried for fifteen minutes, which is right on the edge of running out of time. On the outside, the rescuers had known they were getting close. They just wanted to make sure they reached Eckland before he ran out of air. Once they saw Doc alert and start digging faster, they knew they were in the right area. "Just before Doc found Jeff, his tail was spinning like a propeller," said Paradysz. "I could tell that Doc was really adrenalized. He got a lot of hugs and pats all around. Later on, Jeff threw a party for him."[§]

Eckland suffered a broken back and several broken ribs, but he recovered fully.

"I owe my life to that dog," said Eckland. "I was folded up backwards by that slide and couldn't move. I was buried against a tree and was close to blacking out when I felt his paw hit my back. Without Doc, it probably would have been several hours before they found me, and I'm pretty sure I would have died."[¶]

To show Doc and Paradysz just how

grateful he was, Eckland had Doc's picture tattooed on the left side of his chest.

*Alameda Newspaper Group, February 13, 1999.
†Ibid.
‡Susan Reifer, "Buried Alive," *Skiing Magazine*, January 2000.
§Alameda Newspaper Group.
¶Ibid.

spite distractions, the dogs enter a foster home where their formal training begins.

An ad placed by the National Disaster Search Dog Foundation sums it all up in the Pledge:

> *If you are ever trapped under a ton of rubble, I promise to sniff you out.*
> *I promise to be worth every cent of the $10,000 that it took to train me.*
> *I promise to ignore all other more fascinating smells and concentrate on the scent of live humans.*
> *I promise to go about my work with a wagging tail, even if my paws get sore.*
> *I promise never to give up.*

HOW THEY SEARCH

Human beings shed thirty thousand to forty thousand dead skin cells each day, as well as bacteria and stray hair. A trained search dog needs to be able to identify only a few cells that belong to a person to be off and running.

There are three different ways a SAR dog is trained to find a person: tracking, trailing, or air-scenting. Tracking and trailing are similar: "The dog sniffs a scent article and follows the way the person walked, leading the handler to the subject," said Eva Briggs, a SAR volunteer in New York State who works alongside a Border Collie named Boomer.[4]

"It doesn't matter where the scent comes from," said Cindy Terrell, a member of the California-based Sierra Search Dog team, who partners with a black Lab named Tigger. "It could come from a hairbrush, a pillowcase, or the beer can you drank [from] last night."[5]

A *tracking* dog follows a scent by sniffing the ground, specifically the footsteps of the missing person; a scent article is not necessarily used if it's known exactly where the person last stepped. Police tracking dogs are often used to look for suspects in this fashion.

A *trailing* dog also follows a scent but doesn't necessarily pursue the exact path of the missing person, since a person's scent may not follow the same path due to even slight wind. Trailing dogs are used when an item that belonged to the lost person is handy; an article of clothing or grooming tool works best. The dog is introduced to the scent and then the handler directs him to find the person the scent belongs to. If a personal item is not available, the handler can press a piece of gauze to a chair where the person sat, and that's enough for the dog to go on.

An *air-scenting* dog lifts his head to detect a scent that's airborne, and is most often used over broad expanses of remote wilderness areas or in environments with snow and water where there are few human scents. This dog is trained to alert at any human scent he finds — which may or may not belong to the missing person — when the lost person's belonging is not available. This dog is trained to follow what's known as a scent cone, a spherical amalgam of human scent that most often takes shape downwind of a person. Once the dog locates the scent cone, he follows its trail until he finds the person it belongs to. Of course, a dog may find the traces of many different people who have passed through the search area in the last week, so in order to narrow it down a little, the search dog will sniff all the humans on the search team in order to eliminate their scents. Then he is directed to look for a human scent that is unfamiliar to him.

Because air-scenting dogs can work in areas of up to forty acres, they usually work without a leash and are trained to respond immediately to the handler's commands, most often spoken or hand signals. What's particularly remarkable is that it's possible for dogs in each specialty to track a scent that is more than ten days old.

And when a tracking, trailing, or air-scenting dog finds the object of his search, he gets his reward, whether it's a favorite toy, food, or effusive praise.

"Every dog works for whatever motivates him," said Briggs. "Boomer's reward is tugging with a toy. So in training, whenever he locates a subject, he gets a big party of praise and tugging."[6]

Although any breed of dog is capable of being trained for search and rescue if he displays standard traits of persistence and patience, some breeds excel in one search discipline over another. Most German shepherds do best as air-scenting dogs while Labs and hounds tend to work best as tracking dogs.

The weather and time of day can help improve a canine SAR's abilities. "Dogs are used a lot at night," says Misty Libby, the founder of the Maine Wilderness K-9 Search and Rescue team. "There's not as many people around at night, so it makes it easier to zero in on a scent."[7]

Rain is also a good thing for SAR since the humidity and wet weather help the scent to hug the ground. However, at the same time, too much rain can easily wash away the scent. Cold weather helps since cool air traps scents closer to the ground. For this reason, many wilderness searches are conducted at night or at least after the heat of the day lessens. But warm weather can make searches easier since more sweat means more cells dispersed, giving a search dog more of a chance to find a person.

Angela Eaton Snovak, a veteran SAR team member in Evergreen, Colorado, and the author of *Barron's Guide to Search and Rescue Dogs,* recommends that SAR teams train a minimum of twenty hours each week. "We tell people to train as often as possible, four to six times a week is great," she said. "We tell people that this becomes their priority in life. If you have small children or a job that needs to be your priority, you need to rethink doing this."[8]

"You have to do this purely for the love of the job because you're not going to profit from it," added Debbie Triplett, an Ohio Task

Force One member who works alongside a dog named Rushton. "In fact, it's going to cost you dearly. It really consumes your life, you have to dedicate so much to it."[9]

It's estimated that it requires about six hundred hours of active practice to fully train a SAR dog. Because there are so many different kinds of search-and-rescue disciplines and the degree of training for each one can consume hours each day as well as weekends, in many cases a SAR dog is trained in just one specialty.

URBAN DISASTER SEARCH

While all urban police and fire departments have K-9 units trained in basic search functions as well as either drug and bomb detection, when the disaster is on a larger scale — such as in the aftermath of a hurricane or earthquake — local rescue organizations call the Federal Emergency Management Agency, which has a network of task forces with highly trained dog-and-handler teams all across the nation who can drop everything and head out to help. In fact, these teams are so highly trained that some regard them as the canine equivalent of elite Navy SEAL squads.

Before being certified as a FEMA canine SAR team, both dog and handler must pass a number of tests that include basic obedience skills and agility. The dog must also prove he can navigate several obstacle courses that mimic what is often found at urban disaster sites: walking over rubble and building wreckage that is typically unstable, climbing up an eight-foot ladder placed at a forty-five-degree angle, navigating across a narrow board situated up to eight feet above the ground, crawling through a dark tunnel where the exit is not visible, and making his way across a rickety section of debris.

"Their playground could kill them every day," said Triplett.[10]

FEMA is split up into twenty-eight regional task force teams scattered across the country, ready to deploy at a moment's notice. However, the dogs are so important to the agency's mission that a team is required to have a certified search dog pair — one dog and one handler — in their jurisdiction before they can respond to an emergency. And with only two hundred certified search dogs spread among the twenty-eight teams, a vacancy can sometimes be difficult to fill, therefore sidelining the entire team. In fact, besides doctors, FEMA-certified dogs are the most difficult positions to fill on a task force, which consists of two thirty-one-person teams and four dogs.

Once a dog is screened and passes all initial tests, intense training begins, usually when the dog is between eighteen and twenty-four months old. Training for the certification test takes at least a year. When a K-9 team passes, they are required to attend specialized training sessions at least once a month, and once a dog is certified, he's on the team for three years.

The ideal dogs for urban SAR are between four and seven years old; at that age, they have some experience and are at their best both physically and emotionally. Younger dogs tend to be less focused on the search and easily distracted at a disaster scene, while older dogs are starting to experience physical issues that could slow them down.

The right dog also possesses a strong degree of mental fortitude, or nerve strength, which refers to a canine's ability to accept stressful situations and soldier on regardless of noise, distractions, or strangers. "Dogs that search disaster areas require extremely high nerve strength because they often work in rubble piles and other hazardous environments," said Aimee Hurt, cofounder of Working Dogs for Conservation. "They must be able to rest on-site in the midst of bustling activity and contend with people, noises and stressful conditions."[11]

RICKY

There were many Dogs of Courage involved in the search, recovery, and aftermath of September 11, 2001, at the World Trade Center site, but one dog whose small size helped in immense ways was Ricky, a rat terrier who was three years old at the time and also the smallest urban search dog in the country.

Though Ricky lived in Seattle with his owner and handler, firefighter Janet Linker, they headed for New York as soon as they heard about the disaster. They arrived on September 19 and immediately dove into the search, working the night shift when the area was particularly surreal — and dangerous.

Ricky was trained to find the scent of people both alive and dead, but unfortunately by the time the team arrived in New York, Linker realized that they'd be looking only for bodies. Eighteen-pound Ricky treated the task like any other of the rescues and hundreds of practice searches he'd been on. And he had a clear advantage over the other dogs on the scene: He could squeeze into very tight spots in the debris and destruction.

"There were a few situations where we

had to climb underneath metal beams, and the space just kept getting smaller and smaller," said Linker, adding that the search and the entire site proved to be very disorienting to not only herself but also the other searchers.

"It was unrecognizable," she said. "I never saw steps. I never saw handrails. It was rare that you'd find a softball-sized chunk of concrete. The only intact thing was the paper. People would find necklaces, or someone's pager or cell phone. You'd find clothing with nobody in it."

But regardless of the mood of the searchers, Linker and Ricky persevered. And she knows that their efforts paid off. "It's really hard to know exactly how many people Ricky helped find," she said. "I saw them take [the bodies of] a policeman and a firefighter out from areas that we had just searched."

During the ten days she and Ricky spent searching the site, Linker never doubted that, along with the other emergency and rescue personnel on the scene, they were performing an invaluable service. But she never stopped worrying about how the work was affecting her dog. "Sometimes I wonder if the dogs feed off our emotions," she said. "If I'm nervous, my dog is nervous. If I'm upset, my dog is upset. Toward the end, he was just tired of working, tired of the noise, the commotion, the power and construction equipment always running. I've never seen Ricky as mellow as he was when he got home."*

*Caitlin Cleary, "Littlest Search Dog Was Up to Big Task," Seattle Times, October 17, 2001.

A canine's mental fortitude is equally important to an individual waiting for help to arrive. "The dog must be perceived as a hope for rescue, not a threat," writes Alexander Ferworn of Ryerson University, who has studied the use of technology for SAR dogs.[12]

Admittedly, not every breed fits these characteristics. In fact, the ideal FEMA dog is a purebred Labrador retriever, with over 50 percent of certified FEMA dogs of this breed; the rest are a mix of Border Collies, German shepherds, goldens, and Belgian Malinois.

Not only temperament but size is important. While some non-FEMA handlers prefer to train smaller dogs for SAR because it's easier for them to squeeze into small areas to reach people trapped under the rubble of a collapsed building, most handlers — FEMA or not — prefer larger dogs because they tend to have the stamina necessary to bring them through stressful days that could run for twelve hours or more.

Regardless of the breed, a keen, almost overpowering desire to continue with the task obviously helps. "A dog with a high work ethic will begin searching without cues from a handler, continue to work at the cessation of a training exercise, and may appear impatient during periods of rest," said Hurt.[13]

According to FEMA, canines with a high "toy drive" are best for urban SAR, which essentially is one big game of hide-and-seek for the dog. "In training, people run from the dog and hide with the toy, playing with the dog when found. By the time the dog is on a real search, he is looking willingly for trapped people."[14]

"The dog has to be tremendously motivated for their toy," said Sheila McKee of the San Bernardino County Sheriff's Search Dog Team and the Riverside Urban Search and Rescue Team, Task Force 6, who worked alongside a yellow lab named Guinness. "They're obsessed about their toy, and the ideal dog is obsessed with any toy you throw."[15]

A SAR dog with a playful streak is also beneficial, but a successful FEMA-certified dog must be able to turn it off and focus on the task at hand for long periods of time. Any dog who is afraid of heights or exploring new territory that he senses is unsafe won't last long in training or in the field. After all, a dog working on an active search must be calm in very tense environments and perform activities that include climbing, being hoisted on a platform or bucket ten feet or more above the ground, lowered on a harness into a dark space where he can't see the bottom, and most important, ignore loud noises and distractions that include other dogs, sirens, and people.

FEMA-certified dogs work naked, or without vests, harnesses, or collars that search dogs in other environments typically wear during an active search. Most dogs involved in urban SAR don't wear booties despite the presence of broken glass and other damaged building materials. The reasoning: Having something on their feet can make it difficult for a dog to regain traction at an unstable search site. "The dogs often need to perform what is called a 'soft walk' where they splay their paws for maximum traction," says a FEMA report. "Collars and booties can sometimes add to the risk of searching in tight or obstructed spaces."[16]

McKee and Guinness worked at the World

Trade Center site after 9/11. When the phone rang after the attacks, she hit the ground running. "At that point, you drop everything, you leave your job, get the gear for you and your dog to survive for at least 10 days, and meet within two hours," she said. "It's very chaotic. We were deployed on Sept. 11 and on the 13th we started on the pile, but no one was found alive after the 12th."

They slept a few hours a day — if that — and returned home ten days later emotionally drained and physically exhausted. "When you're in the mode, you're very much acting on adrenaline. You're focused, and operating on very little sleep," said McKee. "It's only later when you can reflect on the situation."[17]

WILDERNESS SEARCH DOGS

No matter what part of the world you're located in, it's easy to get lost in the wilderness — vast, untrampled places with few landmarks to help guide you. A child can get lost as well as day hikers and people with Alzheimer's or dementia. Even experienced trekkers can get turned around and spend hours or days trying to find their way out.

When searches are organized to help locate people who are lost in the woods, the best tool to have is a trained wilderness search dog.

"We're called out if there's a large area to be covered," said Misty Libby of Maine Wilderness K-9 Search and Rescue. "One dog can cover 20 acres. It takes thousands of people to do that."[18]

As is the case with urban search and rescue, larger breeds are better for conducting wilderness searches since they have more endurance, tend to be stronger, and can run for long periods of time before exhaustion takes over. Their handlers have to be pretty strong as well, since some searches require that teams camp out overnight in order to save time; that means hauling backpacks weighing forty pounds or more with all necessary food, water, and equipment over miles of often rugged terrain.

Some canine wilderness search teams are surprisingly high-tech. While a typical search leader divides up an area by quadrants, which are then assigned to dog teams that use topographic maps to help guide them, many handlers are equipping their canine partners with GPS-tagged vests so that if they become separated, it will be easy to find each other.

Occasionally, a dog team trained in urban SAR will be called upon to help out in a wilderness search. That's what happened in 2007 when Loki, a German shepherd who works alongside handler Roger Matthews with the Colorado Urban Search and Rescue FEMA task force, showed up to locate two hikers who had been lost for five days in a wilderness area northwest of Rocky Mountain National Park. After detecting their scent from fifteen miles away, Loki and Matthews tracked down the hikers.

WATER RESCUE-AND-RECOVERY DOGS

Dogs trained in water rescue and/or recovery can do their jobs from the bow of a boat, from the shoreline, or while swimming. One famous water dog, a Newfoundland named Mas, lived in Italy, and his owner, Ferrucio Pilenga, actually trained him to ride in a helicopter and then jump into the water at the exact spot where he picked up a scent.

Newfies are generally considered the best breed for water work given their thick coats, webbed feet, and love of the water. They can weigh up to 150 pounds, but many are swift swimmers, moving through the water faster than even Olympic contenders.

There is an important distinction between water rescue and water recovery. In water rescue, the dog is serving in lifeguard mode, assisting his human counterparts. A properly trained dog will bring a lifejacket to a person in the water, help lead a person back to shore, or even tow a boat filled with people safely to shore.

Water recovery dogs have one job: to find a body under the water.

Water recovery is not for every dog — or handler, for that matter. One reason: Not all dogs can be trained to be comfortable — or at least tolerate — being on a boat. But most important, it takes dogs with a special tolerance for delayed gratification, simply because their reward for finding what their handler directs them to find is in most cases a body.

After all, the dog receives his reward — praise, a tug on a toy, or a treat — only once his human rescuers determine that he was right. This can be hard for some dogs, regardless of the breed; unlike SAR dogs who work in urban disaster or wilderness searches, where once their find is confirmed, they get their treat, for water recovery dogs, that reward may take hours to arrive given that scuba divers have to confirm the dog's find. And even then, it's not certain.

"[Water recovery is] so challenging, but it's also the most frustrating," said Julie Weibler, a wilderness SAR handler in Larimer County Search and Rescue in Fort Collins, Colorado. "All you can say is my dog's alerting; there's

BILBO

Most dogs who are certified to perform water rescues are primarily trained to alert on a body, since very few searches result in live people.

In Cornwall, in the United Kingdom, one dog is fully trained not only to help rescue live people from the water but also to warn them about rough currents and safe boundaries for swimming.

Bilbo is a Newfoundland who works alongside his owner, Steve Jamieson, former head lifeguard at Sennen Cove beach, a popular summer attraction. Bilbo took

Photo: Steve Jamieson, www.bilbosays.com

the helm as Britain's sole canine lifeguard in 2005.

"He's an indispensable part of the team," said Jamieson. "If an alert comes in, his ears start twitching and he knows something is on."

But often Bilbo senses danger and takes matters into his own, ahem, paws. On one occasion, Jamieson and Bilbo were fixing some gear on a beach with a few sunbathers. Suddenly, Bilbo's ears pricked up and he ran crashing into the surf toward a couple of swimmers who were all but invisible from the shore. "He ran into the water and swam out to them," said Jamieson. "They weren't in any danger and were just enjoying themselves, but Bilbo was there in case they needed him."*

Bilbo also prevents swimmers from entering the water if he thinks the water is too rough. Local swimmer Lein Snippe said that one day Bilbo blocked her with his body while she was wading into the water. "When I didn't stop, he swam out to show me how hard it was for him to get back," she said. "It was incredible."†

During rescues, Bilbo heads out to swimmers in trouble wearing a harness with a float attached to it. He then swims around them and pushes the float in their direction. Once they take hold of the float, he swims toward shore.

Jamieson has trained Bilbo from the time he was a puppy. The public loves him, and there even was a book written about him: *The True Story of Bilbo: The Surf Lifeguard Dog*. In the spring of 2008, when Bilbo had six solid years of lifeguarding under his belt, the Royal National Lifeboat Institution assumed lifesaving duties for the beach from the town. They told Jamieson that Bilbo could no longer serve as a lifeguard because not only would he fail the resuscitation test but that dogs were not allowed on the beach in Cornwall, despite Bilbo's being credited with saving three lives and pulling countless others out of harm's way in his tenure.

Jamieson and the public were outraged, and they started a campaign to reinstate Bilbo to his job. Thousands signed petitions, and eventually Bilbo and Jamieson were allowed back onto the beach part-time, though Jamieson decided to leave the job in July 2010 to devote his time to educating the public about beach safety.

That same month, both Jamieson and Bilbo were vindicated when the chocolate brown Newfie was named Pet Hero of the Year at a ceremony for the U.K. Boomerang Pet Awards in London.

*Richard Savill and Michael Fleet, "Bilbo, the Doggy-Paddling Lifeguard," *Telegraph* (London), July 25, 2006.
†"Sea Dog's a Life Saver," *Mirror* (London), August 24, 2007.

scent here. But I can't tell if the person's here or if the scent is pooling here. It's a mystery because I can't get to it because of that water medium."[19]

SNOW AND AVALANCHE DOGS

The most popular image of a SAR dog who specializes in rescuing people from snow is a Saint Bernard with a brandy-filled wooden cask around his neck. The truth is a bit different: The dogs who patrol the ski resorts and winter wilderness areas of the world today typically are at least half the size of a Saint Bernard, extremely nimble, and more adept — and focused — on digging out a person than bringing him liquid sustenance.

The most perilous aspect of getting caught in an avalanche is not the snow itself but the objects that get pulled along in its path. A typical avalanche can travel as fast as 185 miles an hour and contain tons of snow as well as trees, rocks, and even other people who have the bad luck to be in the area when an avalanche hits. Like a riptide, an avalanche can be alarmingly disorienting; once it stops, it's sometimes impossible for a trapped person to determine which way is up. Plus, it can be as impenetrable as concrete even if it's only a few feet deep.

That's why the first skills that many SAR avalanche dogs learn are to ride a chairlift and remain calm in a moving helicopter or on a sled pulled by a racing snowmobile. While ski patrollers are able to reach a person in danger quickly on skis or a snowcat, dogs are unable to navigate in deep snow. Some ski resorts have sleds that the skier can pull on the way to reach an avalanche victim, but again, that chips away at precious minutes needed to save a life.

Once at the rescue site, a trained snow dog can pinpoint the exact area before the rescue squad begins digging with shovels and hands, assisted by the dog. Time is of the essence; most dogs can detect a person's scent more than thirty-five feet below the surface of the snow. It's bad enough if a person is knocked unconscious, but it can actually be more dangerous if he's still awake: Panicked breathing and body heat can quickly form a thin sheet of ice around a small air pocket, which can lead to suffocation in as little as fifteen to thirty minutes.

In some cases, avalanche dogs are owned by the ski resort where they're based; in others, ski patrollers train their own dogs and bring them along to work. Labs, German shepherds, and golden retrievers are popular in snow rescue work not only for their easy temperaments but also for their thick coats that insulate them against cold and wind.

CADAVER DOGS

Not all SAR teams are involved in rescue. Some are focused just on the search.

"A cadaver dog specializes in the location of human remains," said Andy Rebmann, a retired Connecticut state trooper who trained Rufus, the state's first cadaver dog, in 1978. "That's the simplest way to put it. They're not looking for a body per se. This is a big game for them."

Instead of teaching the dog to alert in an active manner, like pawing at the ground, a cadaver dog alerts in a passive fashion so as to avoid disturbing evidence. "For example, my dog [lies] down," said Rebmann. "We encourage that a dog does a passive alert such as sit, or stand and bark at the ground. It looks strange but it works — rather than have an active alert, where they actually start trying to excavate down to the scent source, because you're working with a potential crime scene."[20]

The results can be astounding, especially with cold cases where the trail is decades old. In one unsolved six-year-old case, Matt Zarrella, a corporal with the Rhode Island State Police, and several canine partners were able to locate evidence in just twenty minutes.

"Using the dogs we were able to reduce the search area and localize a very small area for divers to search," he said of the case, which consisted of the body of a man who had been beaten, burned, and submerged in a swamp for six years. "The divers then waded into the water until they were about chest deep, felt around and started finding bones."

Like humans, not all dogs are cut out for the work even though they're trained to find a body in exchange for a reward. "What we've noticed over the years is that some dogs will have an aversion to deceased individuals," said Rebmann. "We're not sure what causes it, and it doesn't happen with all dogs."[21]

In the end, cadaver dogs help to bring a small measure of closure to families, and that's what keeps their human partners doing the work. "There's nothing like being able to find a missing person and return them back to their family," said Zarrella. "It's a feeling that goes beyond a reward that could never be measured in dollars and cents."[22]

CHAPTER FIVE:
GUIDE, SERVICE, AND ASSISTANCE DOGS

Of all the canines heralded in this book, perhaps the most visible Dog of Courage is the assistance dog. This canine — who can also be called a guide or service dog — is undoubtedly the one who can make a dramatic difference in the life of a person.

Marcie Davis is a paraplegic who despite her disability has lived an active life — running her own consulting firm, meeting with friends, and traveling — since 1972, when she became disabled. However, it wasn't until a certain Lab/golden retriever named Ramona entered her life in 1993 that she realized how much more she'd be able to do, see, and accomplish.

"Suddenly a whole new world opened up for me," she said. "I had considered myself fairly independent prior to getting Ramona. However, it soon became clear that I really was not independent and there were numerous things I never considered until she came into my life. This same eye-opening experience is reported by many new service dog recipients. All of a sudden the impossible seems possible, and things you thought were out of your reach literally and figuratively are now obtainable. Virtually every area in your personal and professional life can be expanded and explored, including your vocation, travel opportunities, housing options, and transportation."[1]

For kids who receive an assistance dog, the change is no less startling. "A dog helps you make friends," said Karen Shirk of 4 Paws for Ability in Xenia, Ohio, a nonprofit group that trains and places service dogs primarily with children. "If your dog does tricks, other kids want to meet you. Kids will ignore your disability if you've got a cool dog."[2]

The Americans with Disabilities Act (ADA), which dictates legal statutes and recommended standards for disabled people across the United States, defines assistance dogs as "animals that are individually trained to perform tasks for people with disabilities such as guiding people who are blind, alerting people who are deaf, pulling wheelchairs, alerting and protecting a person who is having a seizure, or performing other special tasks. Service animals are working animals, not pets."[3]

Generally speaking, a guide dog is specially trained to help a person who is blind, either partially or fully. "A guide dog is trained to lead a person from point A to point B in a straight line, to stop for all changes in elevation — curbs and stairs — and to lead their partner around obstacles, including overhead obstacles such as tree limbs," said Debra Barnes of Guide Dogs for the Blind, an organization that trains and places dogs.[4]

A hearing dog is just what it sounds like: a dog who helps alert people who are deaf or hard of hearing in their everyday activities. These can include the doorbell, telephone, fire alarm, and other noises that can help them in their daily lives or save them from danger.

Service dogs are trained primarily to help people who face mobility challenges and who spend a majority of their waking hours in a wheelchair.

Obviously, a wide variety of people with a multitude of physical conditions can benefit from having an assistance dog, such as a paraplegic or blind or deaf person. (And while the dogs assisting these people may also be trained to alert and detect a wide variety of medical conditions from diabetes to asthma to allergies, those skills are covered in the chapter on medical-detection dogs.)

In recent years, another type of assistance dog has begun to appear on the scene: a psychiatric service or emotional support dog. These are two different categories: Psychiatric service dogs are true assistance dogs, helping people with severe psychiatric disabilities — from post-traumatic stress disorders to depression and panic and anxiety attacks — perform certain tasks. According to Service Dog Central, an online resource about assistance dogs of all kinds, these can include "helping to provide counterbalance/bracing for a handler dizzy from medication, waking the handler on the sound of an alarm when the handler is heavily medicated and sleeps through alarms, doing room searches or turning on lights for persons with PTSD, blocking persons in dissociative episodes from wandering into danger (e.g., traffic), leading a disoriented handler to a designated person or place, and so on."[5]

Emotional support dogs serve individuals in the same way that therapy dogs help patients in hospitals or nursing homes feel better. But unless the dog is trained and certified by a recognized service dog organization, he will not have the same privileges and entrée as bona fide assistance dogs, which can cause some consternation among

119

people who rely on their dogs to help them cope.

"There is a lot of evidence that animals are major antidepressants," said Carole Fudin, a psychotherapist in New York who specializes in the human/animal bond. "They give security and are wonderful emotional grease to help people with incapacitating fears like agoraphobia."[6]

Service Dog Central defines an emotional support dog as "a dog that provides therapeutic support to a disabled or elderly owner through companionship, non-judgmental positive regard, affection, and a focus in life. If a doctor determines that a patient with a disabling mental illness would benefit from the companionship of an emotional support animal, the doctor writes letters supporting a request by the patient to keep the ESA [Emotional Support Animal] in 'no pets' housing or to travel with the ESA in the cabin of an aircraft."[7]

Sally Conway, deputy chief of the Disability Rights Section in the Office of Civil Rights, U.S. Department of Justice, puts it this way: "Generally speaking, if we're talking about therapy, comfort, emotional support animals — and I think those typically are used interchangeably — those are not going to be service animals under the ADA because they haven't been trained to do work or perform a task for the benefit of an individual with a disability. Typically, emotional support animals by their very presence certainly perform a valuable service, but it's an innate ability. It's their mere presence. It doesn't reach the level of having been trained to do work or perform tasks."[8]

A good example of a psychiatric service dog is Kira, a collie who helps a girl named Susan deal with periodic panic attacks caused by hallucinations.

"Susan began using Kira to do 'reality checks,' discerning from the dog's reactions whether phenomena — like the doorbell ringing or the strangers Susan spotted in a room — were real or something she could safely ignore," said Joan Froling, a trainer with Sterling Service Dogs in Sterling Heights, Michigan. Among other tasks, Kira was trained to turn on the light in Susan's bedroom and then sniff out the various corners, closets, and underneath the bed before giving Susan the green light to enter. "Eventually, she was able to stay home alone, which was a huge step toward independence."[9]

The earliest reports of training assistance dogs date back to the sixteenth century, with a few stories about training dogs to help blind people to perform simple tasks and lead independent lives, though others say people were already doing this in the first century A.D.

Training really got under way in Germany during World War I when schools to train dogs to assist blind people were launched in anticipation of helping returning veterans who had lost their sight during the war.

The first guide-dog program started in the United States in 1929, when Morris Frank founded the Seeing Eye in Nashville, Tennessee. Frank had first lost the sight in his right eye at the age of six and then his left eye a decade later, both due to accidents. At the age of twenty, he'd been blind for four years when he read about the schools throughout Europe. He traveled to Switzerland, where he trained with a German shepherd named Buddy. When he returned to the United States, the pair toured the country showing how dogs could help people, before Frank started the school in 1929. Several other schools followed, including Guide Dogs for the Blind, which launched in Northern California in 1941.

A guide dog leading a blind person has become a common sight in many areas since the 1970s; indeed, guide dogs have helped blind people to overcome the stigma. Once other physical disabilities became acknowledged and talked about, starting in the 1980s, people decided to take a page from Morris Frank's book and train dogs in the specific tasks that would make lives easier and help the disabled acclimate into society better.

The Americans with Disabilities Act, initially passed in 1990 with significant updates incorporated in 2008, defines a disability as one of the following:

- A physical or mental impairment that substantially limits one or more of the major life activities of such individual
- A record of such an impairment
- Being regarded as having such an impairment

Assistance dogs — as well as those who are trained to alert to medical emergencies, as described in Chapter Eight — are also covered under this act. According to the ADA, "Businesses and organizations that serve the public must allow people with disabilities to bring their service animals into all areas of the facility where customers are normally allowed to go. This federal law applies to all businesses open to the public, including restaurants, hotels, taxis and shuttles,

HOGAN AND HANLEY

Alex Elman started her career in the wine industry in 1990 working in sales, packaging, and production. After she lost her sight in her twenties, she continued to work in the business with the help of her first guide dog, Hogan. In 2010, she went out on her own, launching Alex Elman Wines, with her second guide dog, named Hanley. Here, she talks about how her dogs have helped her to do her work.

When Hanley, my yellow Lab Seeing Eye dog, turned his nose away from a glass of wine, I knew something was fishy.

The winemaker swore up and down that it was organic, but when I tasted it, I had my doubts. So I stuck it in front of Hanley, and my suspicions were confirmed when he wouldn't even look at the glass.

Photo: Doug Holt

124

"I know you're using some chemical in here," I told the guy.

His reply: "Well, you know, only when we *really* have to . . ."

To prove my point, I then put a glass of wine that I knew was organic in front of my dog. Hanley sniffed once, sniffed again, and didn't turn his head away.

I never trained Hanley or Hogan — my first Seeing Eye dog, who was half Lab, half golden retriever — about wine at all. They both just picked up on it after spending their every waking hour by my side, whether we're in my New York office or on the road tasting wine and talking to wine-makers.

After all, dogs only turn away when they don't like something. In that way, they're a lot like people; they're only going by their instincts, which is what people do when they ask if being blind makes me better at tasting wine.

I tell them I'm not sure because I didn't lose my sight until I was twenty-seven, and by that time I had already started my career and knew I had a very acute sense of smell and taste from growing up in my mother's kitchen. I do know that being blind has improved my focus, so I can concentrate on what's going on inside the glass instead of being distracted by other things.

I first got into organic wines in 1995, the second year of the Millésime Bio organic wine show in Montpellier. I always felt kind of oogy after wine shows and tastings and just accepted that's the way it was. I probably tasted about sixty wines the first day of the show, and I was surprised that instead of feeling horrible at the end of the day, I felt great. That's when I decided there was something to this organic no-chemical wine thing.

Hanley's traveled all over the world with me, and it's uncanny how he's taken on my preferences. I'm not a fan of new oak, so a few years back when winemakers were overusing new oak, he'd start sneezing whenever we'd walk into a winery or barrel room. And the only time it happened was when there were new oak barrels around.

Despite his nose for wine, Hanley *is* still a dog, albeit one who's a bit off-kilter. Usually when we first walk into a vineyard, I let him off his leash and let him run around. He's especially fond of catching flies. I'll be asking the winemaker serious questions and there's Hanley snapping at flies.

Another time when we were in Spain, I

was talking to a winemaker and Hanley started chasing a cat. Next thing I know, Hanley comes racing back with the cat in full pursuit of *him*. He crashed into us, sending wine bottles flying all over the place.

While being blind may not necessarily help get my foot in the door, one thing's for sure: They don't forget me.

And after they meet Hanley, they *really* don't forget me.

grocery and department stores, hospitals and medical offices, theaters, health clubs, parks, and zoos."[10]

WHAT DOES AN ASSISTANCE DOG DO?

According to Marcie Davis, most assistance dog tasks fall into three categories: basic obedience, service tasks, and public access. "These specially trained dogs assist [with] tasks such as answering the phone or doorbell, retrieving items, alerting to physical problems, carrying items in a pack, assisting their owners while crossing streets, negotiating stairways and elevators, and a host of other daily tasks."[11]

Many assistance dogs wear a vest, tag, or other piece of equipment that identifies them as service animals at work in order to stave off inquiries from store owners and others who may initially protest the entrance of an animal onto their premises. The ID also helps to prevent unwanted pats and touching from passersby, which may distract the dog from his duties. In many cases, a vest also says ASK FIRST BEFORE YOU PET ME, or gives some similar warning.

All kinds of dogs can become assistance dogs, though for some tasks certain breeds and sizes are obviously better suited than others. For instance, dogs who are trained to become hearing-assistance dogs can be small, while Labs, golden retrievers, and German shepherds are favored for guide and service positions because these jobs require size and strength to deal with the myriad tasks required.

The dogs come from different sources, depending on the organization. For instance, Canine Helpers for the Handicapped in Lockport, New York, rescues dogs from shelters or homes that cannot keep puppies. It also accepts purebred dogs donated by breeders. 4 Paws for Ability trains dogs that are donated by owners and breeders as well as shelter dogs, and they also have a small breeding program in-house.

In many parts of the country, the demand

for trained guide and service dogs vastly outnumbers the supply. One reason is cost. Training a dog to become fully qualified and certified as an assistance dog can take up to two years. Plus, there's the initial outlay for a purebred dog if the guide service organization primarily sources breeders for its dogs.

Second, not every dog is cut out for the job. Some estimate that for every successfully placed service or guide dog, fifteen to twenty didn't make the cut for a number of reasons.

According to Canine Assistants, an organization in Alpharetta, Georgia, that trains service dogs for adults and children, there are approximately sixteen hundred people on their waiting list for a dog at any one time. At Canine Assistants, as well as many other training and placement groups, those individuals who demonstrate the greatest need for a dog in their lives automatically get bumped to near the top of the waiting list. Representatives at the group look at the degree of improved quality of life a dog could bring to a person and make a decision based on this criterion. However, even then, the wait could be extended; they estimate that once a person is approved and then moved toward the top of the list, it could still take between one and five years to actually receive a dog.

Before an assistance dog is matched up with a person, a lot of time and money is involved. The vast majority of fully trained service dogs that come from nonprofit agencies are earmarked from puppyhood.

At 4 Paws for Ability, each dog who ends up being placed has undergone approximately 500 hours of training; Jeremy Dulebohn, training director at the organization, says that 120 hours of training is standard in the industry. The investment at 4 Paws is approximately $22,000 in training costs and day-to-day expenses per dog; people who receive a dog typically cover about $13,000 of that amount and the rest is usually taken care of with grants and donations. To date 4 Paws has placed six hundred dogs since the group was founded in 2001, and two hundred dogs are being trained at the facility at any given time.

There are three stages to training: First, the dog lives with a puppy raiser for up to a year, who teaches the dog basic obedience and socializes him. This can take place in a private home or, increasingly, in a prison puppy program, which is covered in Chapter Seven.

Finding people to become puppy raisers can be a challenge, since they know they will

LANDON

When Jerry and Nanette Casha of Allandale, Michigan, decided to accept a nineteen-month-old golden retriever named Landon into their family to help their ten-year-old autistic son, David, they knew their lives would change, but they had no idea just how much the new member of their family would enrich all of them.

In January 2010, they acquired Landon from Paws with a Cause, a nonprofit organization based in Wayland, Michigan, that trains assistance dogs to help people with disabilities all over the country, and from that point on it's been one minor miracle after another, all thanks to Landon.

"Landon helps our conversation skills in our family," says Nanette Casha. "Prior to getting Landon, our conversations with David were very short and revolved around David's

Photo: Gerard Casha

131

needs, and that was it. Now, he'll repeat what we're saying as well as words from TV shows and commercials. As a result, we have better and more interesting conversations in our family."

A side benefit of the improved communication is that David is getting along better with his sister, Molly. Before Landon became a member of the family, David and Molly didn't have much in common. Now the siblings often play together and engage in typical sibling behavior, including teasing, albeit with the help of the dog.

Landon also helps out when it comes to getting David to fall asleep at night, which had always been a big issue. Now, with Landon by his side in bed, David falls asleep almost instantly once Landon plops down. Jerry says that this has helped improve the outlook of the entire family, though he half jokes that he wishes Landon would also help David to sleep in later in the morning. And since David is getting more sleep, the Cashas decided that he could handle a few responsibilities, including making sure Landon eats every day at five o'clock, as well as bathing and brushing him and playing with him in the backyard.

Like other kids his age, David likes to spend time on the computer and play video games, and also like them, if he had free rein to do those activities all day long, he would! Before Landon arrived, David would put up a fight whenever his mom told him to go outside to ride his bike or play. The difference with the dog around is night and day. "It's so much easier," she said. "We tell him it's time to go outside and play with Landon, and the only thing David asks is, 'How long?' Since many autistic kids like to work within strict time guidelines, we tell him that fifteen minutes is good, and he sets the timer and plays with Landon."

Perhaps the biggest advantage is that other kids don't shun him when Landon's around. In the summer of 2011, David attended a YMCA camp with his class. Though he spent most of the time at camp on his own, without Landon — typical policy is for an adult handler to accompany a child and dog and the Cashas wanted David to experience camp by himself without a parent — Jerry and Landon did spend a couple of days at the camp. Suddenly, David was a rock star.

"The other kids went crazy!" said Jerry. "Once they got over the concept of Landon being there, they went back to their own thing. It was really good for David's self-confidence to have that attention."

Even during the time that Landon wasn't present at the camp, David still demonstrated that just having the dog in his life had worked miracles. At the camp, he did the low ropes course, tackled the climbing wall, and even went canoeing, which would have never happened before, since previously he had never liked putting himself in situations where he felt unsteady.

have to give the dog up a year or so later after countless hours of work — and attachment. Brenda Weaver has been a puppy raiser since 2000. "I do hate giving the dogs up, it is horrible, but they are ready for the next step," she said. "You have to think about what difference they will make for their owners and their independence."[12]

Kay Brickner, a volunteer puppy raiser with the Antelope Valley Guide Dog Club in California, agrees. "You go through all the crying and the other emotional stuff, the withdrawals, when your dog gets recalled," she said. "But you get to go to the graduation and see the end product. Now your labor of love will give someone else happiness. It's very rewarding."[13]

Next up is a specialized school, such as 4 Paws for Ability, where the dogs learn to perform the tasks that will help their new owner become independent. Besides a difficult adjustment for the puppy raiser, dogs can also have a hard time since they essentially go from being joined at the hip with their puppy raiser — traveling, sleeping, eating, walking, going to work, and socializing, all necessary to result in a well-trained assistance dog — to being yanked away to attend a school to learn how to do up to a hundred different tasks, from turning on light switches to helping people cross the road and picking up dropped items.

The last stage of training occurs with the new owner. Especially if the recipient has never worked with an assistance dog before, she will typically spend a week or two at the school in order to learn the various commands necessary to live a more independent life.

Occasionally, during training, it becomes clear that a dog will not be an effective assistance dog after all. This can be due to an inability to focus and ignore distractions or to having too much energy for the job. In some cases, unforeseen medical issues arise in the middle of training that weren't previously obvious, like hip dysplasia, cataracts, or severe allergies. Though some will go on to become great family pets — some are adopted by their puppy raisers — others are shifted into training programs for other jobs; high-energy dogs usually go into police or arson work or they're adopted out to search-and-rescue volunteers, where their excessive liveliness is highly valued. And in some cases, these "career-change" dogs are perfect candidates to become residents at a nursing home or nonprofit therapy center.

Some dogs end up being returned after placement because the new owner either wasn't the right match or didn't expect the challenge. "Only one out of 10 dogs that we test qualify for the program, and some people are not accepted as well," said Beverly Underwood, the founder of Canine Helpers. "You have to want to take care of the dog; it's not mechanical."[14]

At 4 Paws for Ability, about 10 percent of dogs end up coming back. "Some fail because parents weren't prepared for how much extra work a dog would be," says Karen Shirk. "They can barely get themselves and their special-needs child out the door. Adding a dog feels overwhelming."[15]

Other times, it's a clear mismatch. Trainers evaluate a dog's personality from the beginning and try to match his energy and temperament with a person who is similar. At 4 Paws, prospective dog owners send Shirk a video of the child so she can gauge the degree of disability and pair up a dog who will work. "A child looks gentle on the video, so we place a soft dog," she said. "But then the child's violent meltdowns scare the dog, and he starts avoiding the child."[16]

Though pairing a child and dog has its challenges, the vast majority of placements work out, which can help open up the world to people who never believed it was possible.

TEAMWORK

It's a common misconception that an assistance dog leads his human. Yet at the same time, it's erroneous that the human gives the orders.

The two work together as a team, and in the beginning it can take a good deal of time for the two to get used to each other. But they both play an equally important role in doing what's necessary to get through each day.

For instance, in the case of a guide dog and his partner, at first the dog doesn't know where to go. So the handler has to tell him "right," "left," or "straight," as the case may be. In time, after the dog learns his human partner's daily routines, the handler will need to say only "grocery store" or "park," and the dog will be able to seamlessly navigate the correct path.

At the same time, since a blind person isn't able to see any obstructions or barriers along the route, it's up to the dog to proceed or to totally disregard the human's commands, especially when it comes to crossing the street. Known in guide-dog circles as selective disobedience, this particular skill is a shining example of how dog and human work together to create one great team.

Steve Drewek, who has cerebral palsy and uses a wheelchair, lives in Green Bay, Wisconsin, with his black Lab Max. Max and Steve quickly bonded and forged a seamless relationship where the dog helped him navigate the city. One day, they were about to cross the street at the Walk signal, but an oncoming car ran through the red light. Max used his body to block Drewek's wheelchair and prevent him from moving right in front of the car. If Max hadn't practiced selective disobedience, Steve would have certainly been severely injured, perhaps even killed.

In some cases, getting a service dog enables a person to live a life that was previously unimaginable. Aaron Ellis, an Iraq veteran suffering from post-traumatic stress disor-

EFRAM

Bob Fliegel of Westfield, New Jersey, is not one to let disability interfere with his life. Indeed, he's essentially forged full speed ahead while people facing far less adversity look for any excuse to stagnate.

Bob was born prematurely in July 1978, which resulted in a severe case of cerebral palsy. "He was diagnosed when he was eight months old, and since then, we have lived in the world of disability," said his mother, Sarah Fliegel, a former social worker. Bob has had numerous surgeries throughout his life and today he uses a wheelchair to get around.

But he hasn't allowed anything to stand in his way. When Bob was young, he was the first student with significant physical disabilities to attend a neighborhood school. He then proceeded to Hofstra University in Hemp-

Photo: Jennifer Pottheiser

stead, New York, where he graduated with a degree in business administration in December 2003.

After graduation, Bob and his mother and father, Les, spent several years traveling extensively throughout the United States; eventually they'd touched down in all fifty states. While he was traveling, Bob decided that he wanted to live as independently as possible, and he realized one path to helping him achieve that kind of life was with a service dog by his side. After being footloose for so long, he was finally ready to make the long-term commitment that a dog required.

He applied to receive an assistance dog from Canine Companions for Independence (CCI), a not-for-profit organization in Santa Rosa, California. After an intensive two-week training period at CCI's northeast regional training center on Long Island, in November 2006 Bob graduated with Efram, a golden retriever–yellow Lab mix. From the day they returned home to New Jersey, Efram showed that he was eager to work and help Bob in a number of ways, physically, emotionally, and socially.

First, the physical: Efram can retrieve television remotes, keys, and eyeglasses. He can jump up to open automatic doors with an "up" and he can "push" or "tug" things with those commands. As a result, Bob no longer needs to rely on other people as much to help him perform his daily tasks.

Efram also helps Bob emotionally. While he was away at college, Bob developed an anxiety disorder. Bob calls Efram when he starts to feel anxious, and the dog immediately puts his head on Bob's knee to comfort him, or sprawls his body across Bob's lap so he can pet him. Having Efram as his partner has reduced Bob's anxiety level immeasurably. In addition, while Bob occasionally focuses on his inner turmoil, he can't stay there for long because he has to step outside of himself in order to care for Efram.

Finally, Efram helps Bob socially in a big way. For one, Bob is much more outgoing than he used to be. Efram's assistance-dog certification allows him to go everywhere with Bob. Without Efram, Bob was pretty much ignored whenever he was in public, or worse, stared at. With Efram by his side, other people constantly want to talk to him, and as a result Bob has become a person with a cool dog.

Today, Bob and Efram volunteer for CCI by doing demonstrations and giving talks about service dogs to the public. Together they visit children at schools and camps and adults at senior citizen centers, hospitals, and rehab centers, and they attend trade shows for people with disabilities to educate them about life with a service dog. They also try to recruit puppy raisers and reach out to people who could benefit from an assistance dog. Bob knew that having Efram would change his life, but he never knew how completely it would change for the better.

der, was one of the first veterans to receive a psychiatric service dog to help him navigate the world; previously, the military assigned service dogs only to soldiers with physical injuries. To Ellis, there is essentially no difference. After Mya arrived in his life, he not only stopped taking his medication but was also able to do things that the rest of us take for granted, like going to a grocery store or even just walking around the block.

"If I didn't have legs, I would have to crawl around," he said. "If I didn't have Mya, I wouldn't be able to leave the house."[17]

Among other skills, Mya can sense if Ellis is having a flashback or panic attack, keep other people away if he starts to feel anxious, and even dial 911 to get help.

The dog also helps reduce Ellis's feelings of isolation and distrust of other people when they approach him to talk about the dog. That, in turn, starts him talking about the war and his life today, which can work wonders in helping him to regain emotional balance.

Indeed, the constant attention is something that takes some time to adjust to, especially for people who previously were pretty much ignored or even ostracized when they went out in public.

"The incessant curiosity [about Ramona] expressed by strangers in public places was especially difficult for me," said Marcie Davis. "When you receive a service dog, you must be prepared to confront the public and to explain to them the proper etiquette regarding the dog. This has been one of the more difficult things for me. Some service-dog recipients place a sign on their dog's backpack or harness. Talking with strangers about your service dog is definitely something you need to be prepared to address."[18]

It's not always easy, but in the end, life with a service dog can definitely work wonders, though it does take some time.

"Over the first year, Ramona and I worked diligently to perfect our routine and to understand each other's habits, likes, and dislikes," said Davis. "It took time, energy, and hard work to completely trust each other. Throughout the first year, there were times when I questioned whether I had made the right decision to get a service dog. I found out later that this is a typical experience after making such a life-altering decision."[19]

Chapter Six:
Therapy Dogs

When it comes to dogs, what's not to love? Especially if you're hurting in some way — physically or emotionally. Even if you don't have a dog of your own, a visit from a canine can work wonders, not only making you feel better but also helping to speed recovery.

Plus, it can be more valuable and effective than other medical forms of treatment that are prescribed by medical professionals.

"The dog can be a distraction to the pain that a patient feels, and also to the rigor or the monotony of the therapy," says Karen LeFrak, who has worked with her poodle, Jewel, at Mount Sinai Hospital in New York. "For one, it provides comfort for those who respond to animals. It also improves movement, speech, and cognitive functioning, all of which can be quantifiable and documented to some extent."[1]

A variety of medical studies confirm that pet ownership, or even regular visits with a canine, can help to lower blood pressure and decrease respiratory issues, while also reducing the levels of stress hormones and increasing the calming hormones. In fact, in one study, titled "Cardiovascular Reactivity and the Presence of Pets, Friends, and Spouses: The Truth About Cats and Dogs," researchers Karen Allen and Jim Blascovich found that when patients were stressed, a dog was more effective than friends in reducing blood pressure and lowering heart rate. Ironically, spouses tend to score lowest; in their presence, blood pressure and heart rate took the most time to return to regular. Another study, from 1980, showed that the survival rates among dog owners recovering from heart attacks were higher than those who didn't have any pets at all.

Even Florence Nightingale recommended the use of animal therapy for her patients. "A small pet is often an excellent companion for the sick, for long chronic cases especially," she wrote.[2]

Pet therapy falls into several different categories. Animal-assisted activity (AAA) involves pets who are not trained to be part of the medical team; they visit with patients, and their mere presence is found to be beneficial. Dogs who work alongside a medical professional like a physical therapist or social worker are working in animal-assisted therapy (AAT). Generally, AAA pets just need to pass basic obedience tests and demonstrate that they're comfortable working with a variety of people and in a number of different, occasionally stressful environments, while AAT dogs are more highly trained so they can work in specific treatment programs.

Two organizations have spearheaded the acceptance of canine therapy: Therapy Dogs International and Pet Partners (formerly known as the Delta Society). Both organizations screen and train people who want to volunteer in dog therapy and offer an advanced-screening seal of approval to hospital and medical staff who know the therapy team is qualified to volunteer. To date, Pet Partners has approved more than ten thousand therapy teams; Therapy Dogs International reports that it has certified over twenty thousand dogs and their handlers.

And though other animals like cats, ferrets, and even birds have become certified in animal therapy, about 95 percent of teams working in pet therapy environments are canine. "Dogs have become so domesticated that they are easier to introduce into a wide variety of settings," said Amy Rideout, president of HOPE Animal-Assisted Crisis Response, a nationwide group based in Eugene, Oregon,

Sigmund Freud is known for many things, including being the father of psychoanalysis, but one little-known fact is that he was a dog lover who often employed the services of his chow, Yofi, in his analysis work with patients.

In fact, he thought dogs were clearly superior to humans in many ways, one of which was that they possessed a sixth sense that made it possible for them to alert to a person's real motivations instead of what he or she said aloud in therapy sessions. He relied on Yofi not only to help him to tune in to his patients' analysis better but also as a soothing distraction, so that patients could pet the dog's head, and more often than not, be inspired to talk about what was really troubling them instead of skating around on the surface of their emotions.

Though Yofi usually lay under Freud's desk during sessions, she often sidled up to the patient; Freud, in turn, would interpret the dog's position in the room to gauge a patient's emotional condition. The more tense a patient was that day, the farther away the dog; if he or she was calm that day, Yofi would lie close to the couch. And some have reported that he relied on Yofi's inner clock; she would officially announce that a session was over by scratching at the door or by yawning and stretching, never allowing Freud to exceed the hour by even a minute.

Freud didn't get his first dog, a chow named Lun-Yu, until he was well into his seventies. He had Lun-Yu for only a little over a year when the dog ran away and was found dead. Within a short time, he obtained Yofi, and by the sound of things, he was really caught off guard by the intensity of the emotion in the relationship between them.

"One can love an animal like [Yofi] with such extraordinary intensity, the beauty of an existence complete in itself," he wrote. "Often when stroking Yofi I have caught myself humming a melody which, unmusical as I am, I can't help recognizing as the aria from *Don Giovanni:* 'The bond of friendship / Unites us both.'"*

"Dogs love their friends and bite their enemies," he continued, "quite unlike people, who are incapable of pure love and always have to mix love and hate in their object relations."†

Freud had been diagnosed with cancer when Yofi came on the scene, and the dog served as a soothing balm to the pain of the disease and treatments he had to endure as well as when they were separated. "I miss her now almost as much as my cigar," he wrote while they were apart. "She is a charming creature, so interesting in her feminine characteristics, too, wild, impulsive, intelligent and yet not so dependent as dogs often are. . . . [And] what sympathy she shows me during these hellish days, as if she understood everything."[‡]

Yofi died on January 11, 1937, and Freud was devastated. "Apart from any mourning, it is very unreal, and one wonders when one will get used to it," he wrote in a letter to his friend, the novelist Arnold Zweig. "But, of course, one cannot easily get over seven years of intimacy."[§]

---

[*]Richard John Neuhaus, "Wittgenstein Found Freud Both Alluring and Misleading and Credited Him with Having Produced 'A Very Powerful Mythology,' " *First Things: A Monthly Journal of Religion and Public Life,* April 1, 2008.

[†]Melinda Beck, "Beside Freud's Couch, a Chow Named Yofi," *Wall Street Journal,* December 21, 2010.

[‡]Susie Green, "Freud's Dream Companions," *Guardian* (Manchester), March 22, 2002.

[§]Ibid.

that refers crisis response dog-and-handler teams throughout the country.[3]

The use of animals in therapy has been around for several centuries. The first recorded instance of pet therapy for emotionally disturbed and mentally ill people occurred in the 1700s in England at an institution known as the York Retreat, where a number of animals, including cats and dogs, roamed around outside. Patients were often encouraged to visit with the pets when they ventured outside; their caretakers thought that this reduced the incidence of outbursts and helped the environment as a whole remain calmer.

Later on, in the nineteenth century, as a way to counteract the typically substandard conditions at mental institutions, government officials with the British Charity Commissioners drew on the experiences at the York Retreat and strongly recommended that animals be kept on the grounds at Bethlem Hospital and other institutions to serve as companionship for the patients as well as to make asylums feel more homelike and less like prisons. "There is fondness manifested for pet birds and animals, cats, canaries, squirrels, and greyhounds," wrote a correspondent in the *Illustrated London News* in March 1830. "Some [patients] pace the long gallery incessantly, pouring our their woes to those who listen to them, or, if there be none to listen, to the dogs and cats."[4]

In the United States, pet therapy has been around since the beginning of the twentieth century, its roots cemented in war. St. Elizabeth's Hospital in Washington, D.C., first began to bring dogs and cats into treatment with World War I veterans in 1919, and later, during World War II, staff at the Pawling Army Air Force Hospital in New York State encouraged patients with PTSD and/or physical injuries to help out on the farm located on hospital grounds. Helping feed and care for the horses, cows, and other livestock, as well as the barn cats and farm dogs, was believed to be therapeutic, though the program ended once the war was over.

The first recorded use of dogs in private therapy environments was in the early 1960s when Boris Levinson, a child psychiatrist in New York, observed that patients tended to respond better to treatment when Dr. Levinson's dog, Jingles, was in the room during appointments. Levinson coined the term "animal-assisted therapy," and he would go on to write the first books on the subject: *Pet-Oriented Child Psychotherapy* and *Pets and Human Development.*

Nursing Homes and Hospitals

Gus, a five-year-old Great Pyrenees, likes his job so much that he actually has two of them: one at Good Samaritan Hospital in Dayton, Ohio, and the other at Carriage Inn of Dayton Nursing Center. According to his owner, Sandra Tomlinson, Gus takes his job so seriously that he willingly endures a bath prior to every hospital visit. As owners of this double-coated breed know, this can be no small feat.

But Tomlinson says Gus puts up with it because he loves his job so much. On one hospital visit, he took a shine to one female patient. "This lady had no one to visit her and we went in there for that purpose and Gus knew it," said Tomlinson. "This lady has several children, but their work and families don't allow them to be with her right now. Dogs can sense that kind of loneliness in a voice, and Gus knew she needed the company."[5]

Some nursing homes also have resident live-in therapy dogs. At Marriott's Brighton Gardens in St. Charles, Ohio, Logan, a golden retriever, and his friend Sadie, a black cat, are permanent residents and staffers who essentially put themselves on call 24/7. "Logan is very special," said special care manager Jean White. "He's been [in the special care unit for Alzheimer's residents] for probably two years, and he's basically a pet for everybody. Everyone takes ownership of him. If someone is depressed, he puts his head in their lap. I've even seen him lick someone who has fallen asleep, in order to wake them up."

Besides offering basic companionship, Logan provides an even more important function. "He notifies us when someone comes back here [into the unit] who isn't normally here, or shouldn't be back here," said White. "He keeps our residents safe. He's our eyes and ears. If a resident is in their room and is having a problem, he alerts us. If someone is walking down the hall, Logan brings us to them. He's really something special."[6]

Even though many nursing homes and senior residential centers require that a dog be certified by Pet Partners or Therapy Dogs International in order to visit, not all visiting dogs fall into that category. At the Michaelsen Health Center in Batavia, Illinois, in addition to a resident rabbit named Thumper who regularly visits with patients, dogs often show up to just provide companionship. "One staff member brings her dog in once a month," said Michelle Miklosik, assistant activity director at the center, who adds that occasionally relatives visiting patients can also bring well-behaved dogs with them. The visits help spread goodwill throughout an entire wing, even if a resident just spots the dog strolling by outside the room.

"The socialization is a benefit," she said. "These animals bring back memories of [the residents'] own pets. The love and the smiles on their faces are the biggest benefit."[7]

Owners and staff often comment on how remarkable it is that a dog not only knows who needs companionship most but also what she needs to do. "If a resident is having an off day, she just goes and sits with them," said Christy Johnson, recreation/therapy director at Parmly LifePointes in Chisago City, Minnesota, of her golden retriever therapy dog, Maddie. "We've seen dementia patients remember her name. These types of things are not supposed to happen. They don't remember our names, but dementia patients [will] call out her name."[8]

There are other benefits as well. "We found that people who had spent time with a therapy dog were calmer during tests than those who hadn't," said Dr. Richard Ruchman, chairman of radiology at Monmouth Medical Center in Long Branch, New Jersey.[9]

And when it comes to the end of life, therapy dogs can provide an important function. "Having [a dog] in the hospice facility is probably more beneficial to the patients' families than to the patient themselves, who are often so medicated or so sick that they are unable to appreciate visitors in the room," says Michelle A. Rivera, author of *On Dogs and Dying: Inspirational Stories from Hospice Hounds*.[10]

Sara Roby is an animal-assisted therapist at VITAS, a hospice in Broward County, Florida, and she often employs her Yorkshire terrier, Taiko, in her work. "People who are visiting patients are there for very long days," she says, adding that she notices an immediate shift as soon as she brings Taiko into a patient's room. "The family will play with him for a while and then say, maybe, well, let's go to lunch or something. They can break away from the dog easier than they can break away from sitting vigil at a loved one's side. It shows them that even though they are going through this terrible time, they can still laugh, even have a good time, even while they are experiencing this anticipatory grief. It's an amazing thing."[11]

Physical and Occupational Therapy

Dogs of Courage who serve as therapy dogs can also help people recover more quickly by working as AAT dogs with their human partners. At Community Hospital in Munster, Indiana, Titus, a Great Dane, is a certified therapy dog and serves as assistant to his owner, Jill Armstrong, a senior physical therapist and the coordinator of the Animal Assisted Therapy program at the hospital. But Titus doesn't discriminate; he puts in a full day helping the other speech, occupational, and physical therapists on staff.

"If we tell a patient who either isn't motivated to walk or has difficulty with ambulation, 'Let's take a walk with Titus,' suddenly the patient is empowered because they're getting to walk with the dog," says Armstrong. "The repetitive task of walking is more interesting, fun, challenging, and motivational with Titus." The Great Dane also helps kids who are attending speech therapy sessions at the hospital. While a human speech therapist may have trouble getting a child to read aloud from a book for a speech evaluation, Titus experiences no such resistance. "Children will read to a dog because they feel a dog will not judge them if they get a word wrong," Armstrong said. "Plus, it's fun for kids to have a dog present during their therapy session."[12]

When called upon to help people who are in therapy regain function after a stroke, Titus waits patiently while a patient in occupational therapy squeezes a ball and then throws it across the room. It doesn't matter how far — or near — she throws the ball, he eagerly retrieves it and drops it in her lap so they can do it again. Armstrong also gets help grooming the dog, since brushing Titus exercises a weakened arm. Sometimes patients help by fastening the buttons and zippers on his vest or by buckling and unbuckling Titus's leash.

Sometimes, just a pat on the head is a huge achievement for a patient, especially for stroke victims who are paralyzed on one side of the body. The simple act of petting a dog over and over not only helps the patient to relax but also performs the same function as a more tedious standard PT exercise. "[Dogs] make our jobs so much easier," said physical therapist Lori Senft of Henry Mayo Newhall Memorial Hospital in Valencia, California. "Dogs are a good motivating factor to get patients to do more. They distract them from thinking of their pain and change their attitude."[13]

And not surprisingly, just as dogs help the family members of hospice patients feel better, staff members at hospitals and other medical establishments benefit too. Darlene Fraschetti often volunteers at Mayo Newhall with her dog, Keesha, a black English cocker spaniel, whose tail starts wagging as soon as they enter the facility and doesn't stop until they leave. "We call that her happy meter," said Fraschetti, who adds that the nurses often clamor for some time with Keesha as well. "We find that the staff enjoys our visits as much as the patients do," said Fraschetti. "It's a stress reliever for them."[14]

Kids: At-Risk, Special Needs, and Reading

The most poignant and noticeable results come when therapy dogs work with children. After all, dogs and kids share many traits: their size, their vulnerability, and their total ability to trust, at least when still pretty young.

"For a child whose heart may have been broken, having that unconditional love and interaction with a creature that's not judging them is so powerful," said Amanda Graham, program supervisor at the Midwestern Colorado Center for Mental Health in Gunnison. "Animals give complete, instant feedback. They don't mince words. They don't lie. Most children don't either. They operate on levels that are very much alike."[15]

Amy Pickett is a mental health therapist at the health clinic at Sheridan Middle School in Sheridan, Colorado, and works alongside her canine partner, Basil, a golden retriever.

Pickett marvels at Basil's unfailing ability to listen to kids. "Basil hears many different types of stories," she said. "He gets lots of kids who have experienced a lot of trauma, and they're more comfortable talking with him."

The retriever is also skilled at inadvertently teaching kids how to keep their boundaries and not crowd others. Pickett gives the example of asking a kid to teach Basil a trick.

"I'll ask a kid to teach Basil to sit and work with him teaching him tricks, which Basil of course already knows," she said. They'll follow through, but sometimes their actions prevent the dog from following their instructions. "If they try to crowd Basil, he won't do what they ask, and that parallels their everyday life." Plus, Basil helps ease the tension with the parents of the children she works with. "When parents come in, and they're experiencing stress, they'll pet Basil and they'll feel much more comfortable and at ease talking to me."[16]

Special Needs

Though dogs can serve as full-time guides to individual children with special needs, a topic that is covered at length in Chapter Five on service and assistance dogs, they often help out on a part-time basis with special-needs schoolchildren who benefit from the presence of a furry creature who is patient and doesn't judge. Scout is an English yellow Lab who works with his owner, Nancy Jo Connell, a speech-language pathologist with the Missoula County Public Schools district in Montana. They work together with autistic children at the Jefferson School in Missoula.

Scout's particular talent is to respond with a short, soft bark whenever a child who has trouble with communication skills successfully "talks" with him in any fashion, through words, signs, or symbols. For instance, when a child with a speech impediment correctly uses a word or sentence, Scout responds, with a little prompting from Connell. Similarly, when an autistic child says even one word, Scout again gives an encouraging bark. If a deaf kid successfully signs, again Scout helps out with a response.

Connell has seen firsthand the positive effects that Scout provides. Before she showed up in his class, one boy with autism rarely spoke. "He talks very little, but the first day that Scout came, he said 'puppy' for the first time," said Connell.

And if a student makes a mistake, instead of replying in some way, Scout merely remains silent. "It's not a corrective model," said Connell. "We don't tell them what's wrong.

APOLLO

Laura Berton-Botfeld didn't know what was in store when she and her apricot standard poodle named Apollo started volunteering as a therapy dog team at UCLA Medical Center. She thought she and her canine partner would be able to bring some small dose of cheer to people staying at the hospital, but she couldn't predict that Apollo would actually prove to be the pivotal point in steering a little girl's recovery.

One day after they had been volunteering for several months, they were in the Mattel Children's Hospital when a man walked directly toward them. Something in his approach was a bit stressed and concerned. He pointed at Apollo and asked if he was a therapy dog. Laura replied that indeed he was, and the man requested their services, explaining that Sophia, his ten-year-old daughter, was in the ICU.

Laura hesitated; were dogs allowed in the wing with expensive medical equipment, not to mention the delicate condition of most of the patients? She asked a doctor nearby if it was okay — meanwhile the father seemed impatient for her to follow along — and once the physician gave his blessing, they gingerly entered the room.

Inside the darkened room filled with tubes and equipment and monitors that buzzed and beeped, she and Apollo approached the bed. The father explained that the little girl had bacterial meningitis and had been in a coma for more than two weeks and that the doctors weren't holding out much hope.

As her eyes adjusted to the darkness, Berton-Botfeld saw that the girl's eyes were open but unseeing, staring at nothing. "Seeing her like that was more than I had anticipated, and I didn't know if I could face this situation," she said. "But I looked at my dog, brave and valiant as ever, and he gave me a burst of strength."

Apollo approached the bed and gave a gentle sniff. The little girl's father placed his daughter's hand on the dog's head while he whispered repeatedly, "There's a dog named Apollo here."

Suddenly, the energy in the room changed and Apollo did something he'd never done before. "Apollo seemed to stare into the deep abyss of her beautiful but blank blue eyes," she remembered. "For a moment, there was definitely some strange sort of connection between the two.*

"It was the weirdest thing," she said. "[The girl's] eyes seemed to just lock onto Apollo's, and the dog's gaze was so intense I thought he was going to kiss her — something therapy dogs are trained not to do."†

Apollo stared at the girl for about twenty minutes while the adults looked on. But the little girl didn't respond; her big blue eyes remained unseeing. After a while, the therapy team left the room to visit other patients, but Laura kept thinking of how her dog had reacted in the presence of the comatose girl.

About an hour after they left her room, Laura's cell phone rang. Jack Barron, the director of UCLA's volunteer animal-therapy team, was on the other end with shocking news. "He said, 'Sophia just woke up,'" recalls Laura. "'And her first words were, "Where's Apollo?" How fast can you get back here?'"‡

A month later, Sophia was back at home. Laura spoke with her on the phone. "She told me that Apollo was the only memory she had from her coma experience. All she remembered was being surprised to see a dog's face right in front of hers, and it made her want to laugh but no sounds would come out. Her next memory was of waking up."[§]

*Laura Berton-Botfeld, "The Healing Medicine of a Wet Nose," *UCLA Medicine Magazine,* Winter/Spring 2012.
[†]Ellen Michaud, "Therapy Dogs and Healing," *Saturday Evening Post,* November/December 2011.
[‡]Ibid.
[§]Berton-Botfeld, "The Healing Medicine of a Wet Nose."

If they say a word and Scout doesn't respond, we say, 'Oh, he doesn't understand you.' The single most important thing he does is show these kids the power of communication."[17]

Reading

Dogs can help students to become better readers as well. In hundreds of programs across the country, students who have trouble reading are boosting their ability by reading books aloud to a dog.

Animal Reading Friends — also known as ARF — is a special class for second and third graders at Travis Elementary in San Marcos, Texas, where students work on improving reading and comprehension by reading books aloud to two therapy dogs named Magellan and Moses. Once each week, volunteer handlers Julie and Kevin Romig visit Leanna Duesterheft's Title 1 reading class with their specially trained Reading Education Assistance Dogs (READ). Students take turns reading aloud to each dog for about twenty minutes after the dog decides which book he'd like to hear that day, when the student spreads out several books for the dog to choose from. Depending upon that week's curriculum, Magellan and Moses pick out a book by responding to a prompt from Julie or Kevin.

"I've heard comments such as, 'Magellan will like this book because it's about a cat,' or 'This book talks about treats. Moses will get excited when he hears that word,'" said Duesterheft. "All students have shown more confidence when reading and are having conversations about books for the first time. We have seen the students more motivated and have actually seen improvement in attendance for at least one student who was having problems with absences."

Instead of sitting at a desk, dog, handler, and student go off to a quiet corner of the classroom where they can lounge on pillows or a bean-bag chair. The handler is trained just like the dog, to ask children questions as they read, or to prompt for more information. Sometimes in the middle of a reading session,

Julie or Kevin will tell a student that "Moses has never heard that word before. Can you tell him what it means?" And both dogs will perform appropriate tricks, like staring at the page to make it appear as though they're paying rapt attention or turning a page with a paw.[18]

Psychological Therapy

One of the reasons that Boris Levinson, the founder of pet-facilitated therapy, believed so strongly in using animals during therapy sessions with patients is that he thought people became increasingly stressed the more isolated they were from the natural world. "One of the chief reasons for man's present difficulties is his inability to come to terms with his inner self and to harmonize his culture with his membership in the world of nature," Levinson wrote. "Rational man has become alienated from himself by refusing to face his irrational self, his own past as personified by animals." He believed that pets "represent a halfway station on the road back to emotional well-being."[19]

Given the therapeutic nature of the mere presence of a dog in hospitals and other medical establishments, it's no wonder that more professionals in the mental health field bring their dogs into their practice as a matter of course. Often, all they have to do is sit alongside a patient; many psychologists, psychiatrists, and social workers can attest to the power of healing by merely having a dog in the room.

In most cases, they are not trained as AAT dogs. New York–based psychiatrist Drew Ramsey is accompanied to his office by his shih tzu, Gus, who is better than Ramsey at picking up on the cues patients send as to what they need and either snuggles up on the sofa next to a patient or sits quietly on the floor.

A dog can also pave the way for people to open up about their problems. If a patient becomes uncomfortable talking about a certain subject or memory, he'll often block out the other human in the room and tell his story to the dog instead. Gus provides another very important service that is unfortunately in short supply during therapy sessions. "We can't hug patients, but patients can hug Gus," said Dr. Ramsey, who now considers the dog one of the most important tools in his arsenal. "I think about Gus the way a cowboy thinks of his horse: he's part of the job."[20]

Having a dog in the room also means that therapy can progress much faster than normal and serve as a vital prompt. Lois Abrams is a therapist in Los Alamitos, California, who brings Duke and Romeo, her two Cavalier King Charles spaniels, to the office with her. In one session, Dr. Abrams wasn't aware that a patient was suffering from depression until Duke sat next to the woman. However, she knew from sessions with previous patients that Duke tended to stay on the floor when around people with anxiety issues but knew that those who are depressed welcome closer contact. So she took her cue from the dog. "When I asked if she was depressed, suddenly the woman poured out her heart to me," said Dr. Abrams. "My three-year-old dog knew more than I did."[21]

And when a psychologist with a canine is working with a patient who is overly aggressive or has trouble controlling impulses, the dog can serve as a barometer. "The animal will stay near that person until the person starts upsetting the animal, and then they'll move away," said Bill Kueser, vice president of marketing at Pet Partners. "The doctor then can point out the effect the patient's behavior had on the animal. They seem to be able to work through aggression issues more effectively that way."[22]

The Unexpected

Dogs are providing beneficial therapy in a number of places you wouldn't expect.

For one, how about a church? At Holy Cross Lutheran Church in Portage, Indiana, Pastor Tim Engel brings his golden retriever, Fuerst, to work every day. "His job is to help open up opportunities for conversations and Christian ministry that otherwise wouldn't happen," said Engel. "If the dog provides comfort for people and is something that makes them feel more at ease then he's doing his job." Though the dog is always nearby when parishioners or other staffers come into his office for advice or just to chat, Fuerst also accompanies Engel when he makes rounds at nearby hospitals and nursing homes.

But the one place where he's perhaps noticed the most is on Sundays during the weekly church service. "Not everybody sees the value of Fuerst like I do," he said. "But the majority of the members look forward to seeing him on Sunday morning and they understand his function in our church."[23]

Surprisingly, Fuerst is not unusual, at least in the Midwest; Lutheran Church Charities has helped to place almost thirty golden retrievers in special K-9 Parish Comfort Dog Ministries in Indiana and Illinois.

A courtroom is another venue where the sight of a dog can generate some surprised looks. But the truth is that, at least in Florida, a dog can provide an extremely important service. A number of volunteer handlers and their certified therapy dogs work with the Pet Therapy in the Courts Program in the Second Circuit known as ComForT Dogs — Companions for Therapy. A dog sits alongside while a child talks to a judge or a victim testifies about a violent crime.

"Our role is to spend time with the victim while they are either waiting to do a deposition or go into court and testify, knowing they are going to have to see the abuser," said Tallahassee lawyer Bobbie Jo Finer, who works with her dachshunds Piper Laurie and Honey Girl. Once Honey Girl sat in the lap of a fourteen-year-old girl while she testified about sexual abuse. "She sat there with Honey Girl in her lap, and I sat quietly nearby holding Honey's leash," said Finer. "The young woman stroked her the whole time she was giving testimony. This little dog helped her relax. It helped her get through it."

So far, neither prosecution nor defense lawyers have complained. "People see they are getting better testimony, and it's a good thing for both sides," said Finer. And judges also see the invaluable service that the dogs provide.[24]

"The dogs really, really help relax the kids and give them something to have fun with and occupy them while they are waiting to come into the courtroom," said Judge Jill Walker, a family-court judge in Wakulla County, Florida. "The result is that when I get people coming into court, they are not loaded for bear. It makes my job easier. It gives me an entryway, and we talk about the dogs. I'll ask: 'Which dog do we have in the hall today? Did you like the dog?' And they see I'm not the judge from the old-timey movies that they need to be afraid of."[25]

Dogs can also be found in schools, but for more than helping kids to read, and for a slightly older demographic. In Phoenix, a therapy dog named Ella who usually visits sick people in hospitals has expanded her reach; several times a year, her handler, Diane Alexander, brings her to ease the suffering of students studying for final exams at the law school at the University of Arizona.

"The students love it," said Alexander. "They spend so much time with their noses in books or staring at a computer. Hugging a dog for a little while, it makes them feel happy."[26]

CAN YOU AND YOUR DOG BECOME A THERAPY TEAM?

It can be very rewarding to serve as a canine therapy team, seeing people instantly brighten when you walk through the door, but it takes time, training, and jumping through hoops before you set out for your first visit to a hospital or nursing home.

It can also be heart-wrenching due to the life-threatening conditions of the patients. Barbara Babikian of Orange County, New York, often volunteers with her sheltie, Lillie, at the Hackensack University Medical Center in New Jersey. One of the rules that handlers must follow is that they cannot talk about the patient's disease with either the patient or family, or the staff. Babikian occasionally has trouble with this rule, particularly when she sees a relative struggling with his emotions in the presence of a sick loved one. "Sometimes it's very hard to hold back the tears, but you do it long enough until you leave," she said. Once, she cried during her ninety-minute drive home after she visited a girl with cancer who was barely six years old. Babikian and Lillie visited the girl regularly. "She ended up being in my life for the next two and a half years until she lost her battle with cancer at the young age of nine."[27]

If you can deal with the emotional highs and lows, the good news is that any size, shape, or breed can become a therapy dog. What's more important is the dog's temperament and personality. "There is no one breed, it's the individual," said Michele Siegel, a New York–based trainer who works with dogs and handlers and evaluates teams for Pet Partners. "[The dog] has to like people and enjoy interacting with people. They have to be able to acclimate to new environments because we visit various facilities."[28]

But just as important is the personality and temperament of the human. "We evaluate both ends of the leash," explains Bill Kueser of Pet Partners.[29]

First, in order to work with Pet Partners or any other organization that certifies and/or refers therapy teams to local hospitals and institutions, dog owners are required to take a handler course, either online or at a local workshop. This is designed to help provide basic information and education, as described by Pet Partners:

- How to tell if both you and your animal are a good fit to be a therapy team
- Preparing yourself and your animal for visits
- Identifying and decreasing stress in your animal
- Animal health and safety
- Special needs of specific client groups

- How to interact with different types of people
- Facility health and safety codes
- Patient confidentiality[30]

Next, the dog must successfully pass a physical veterinary exam, have proof of up-to-date rabies vaccination and other immunizations, and be free of internal and external parasites.

Finally, an in-person test conducted by a skilled trainer will test you and your dog in person to see how you work separately, and then evaluate how you work as a team. First up, the Pet Partners skills test "will show whether the animal can be controlled by the handler and follow basic commands. You will be assessed on how you interact with the evaluator, the evaluator's assistants, the animal, and the environment around you."

Next is the aptitude test, which Pet Partners designs "to simulate conditions you may encounter on a visit. This screening helps determine the most appropriate environment for you and your animal to visit. You will be assessed on how well you interact with the evaluator and evaluator's assistants as you simulate being on a visit. They will be role-playing as though they are in a facility. Your interactions may be in the form of questions, responses to the evaluator and evaluator's comments, eye contact, smiling, head nodding, directing the animal to interact, or other verbal and nonverbal methods of communicating."[31]

New Yorker Kate Fischer describes the test that she and her schnauzer Schnapps took. The dog was required "to be hugged, to be squeezed, to be cried into, to be yelled at, to have things dropped on her, to handle a crowded hallway, loud noises, wheelchairs going by, people bumping into her, and people dropping walkers on her."[32]

If you pass the test, Pet Partners or another organization may conduct further evaluation to determine if visiting adults or kids is a better bet, as well as a certain department. The hospital or particular establishment may help to make the decision, which may also be determined by where the need is greatest. And frequently a dog's main therapy gig will be dictated by its size.

When Babikian brings Lillie to visit patients at Hackensack UMC, the sheltie most often just sits on the patient's bed on a blanket made by other hospital volunteers. "Lillie is a cuddler," she said. "When I visit with her, I place her onto the bed of a patient and she will keep repositioning herself until her body is touching the patient, and then she will

176

TOASTER

After Nancy Gordon experienced a horren-dous car crash in 1992, the clinical social worker's life turned into a nightmare. Her chronic neck and back pain weren't allevi-ated with physical therapy or drugs, but she soldiered on in her private practice. In time, however, the unending pain took its toll, and after she was diagnosed with de-pression, fibromyalgia was next in line. It took her a few years, but she decided the only thing she could do was stop working and accept that she had to go on disability.

Without work and with the pain that never quite went away, it's not hard to understand

Photo: Carol Sveilich, MA,
www.writefaceforward.com

177

why Gordon grew increasingly despondent by 1999. That's when a dog entered her life, and he not only helped ease her pain but also started her in a whole new career direction.

Gordon was visiting a friend who had a Mexican hairless breed of dog known as a Xolo — short for the tongue-twisting Xoloitzcuintli; Xolotl is the Aztec god of fire, lightning, and death, and *itzcuintli* means "dog" in Aztec. The dog climbed into her lap, and though not a dog person, she naturally started petting him.

The first thing she noticed was the dog's warmth. His body felt a lot warmer than any other dog she'd known. Gordon had relied on heating pads to help ease her pain, and so she set her wrist next to the dog's body.

Within fifteen minutes, the pain was gone.

She knew she had to find a Xolo of her own. She researched the breed as well as breeders and discovered that a Xolo's body temperature is the same as that of other dogs — 103° is the norm — but because they have no fur to get in the way, the body heat essentially spills out of them and serves as a direct heat source for anyone close by.

Some medical professionals concur: "Xolos are perfectly suited for soothing joint and soft tissue pains because they easily give off body heat," said Michel Selmer, a veterinarian in Long Island, New York.*

Gordon brought Toaster home not too long after her epiphany and trained the dog to respond to commands like "neck," so that she crawls up to lie across Nancy's neck, or to burrow in against her lower back when she's driving. She even attended a service-dog program so that they would never be separated in public places or on an airplane, and also so Toaster could be of even greater service, like opening a door or picking up an item on the floor.

In time, Gordon decided that other people suffering from chronic pain could benefit from a Xolo, so she founded Paws for Comfort, a nonprofit organization to educate people about the medical and physiological value of Xolos and help place service-trained Xolos with people who need them most.

She likes to say that her mission is "X-CPR," or "Xolos for Chronic Pain Relief."

*Linda Childers, "The Cuddle Cure," *Ladies' Home Journal,* March 2009.

relax and fall asleep. Sometimes that is all someone really needs."[33]

In the end, a therapy dog is all about helping people feel better. "I see miracles here every day," said Jack Barron, the director of the People Animal Connection at the UCLA Medical Center. "People who just wake up. People who start eating. People who finally take their meds. People who are paralyzed and then suddenly move a couple of fingers to wave at a dog."[34]

"I love these dogs," said Coleen Moran, a nurse in the adolescent psych unit at UCLA. "They know when someone needs love. And that's better than any medicine."[35]

Along with Bobbie Jo Finer and her dachshunds Piper Laurie and Honey Girl, Chuck Mitchell volunteers with the Pet Therapy in the Courts program in Tallahassee. His canine partner is Rikki, a golden retriever mix, and though they also volunteer at hospitals and nursing homes, Mitchell says the courtroom visits are where he feels like they have the biggest impact.

"When I get to see my dog make a connection with somebody and help relieve some of their pain or stress even for a few minutes, and light up their face, who wouldn't want to be Santa Claus giving out a bag of smiles?" he asks. "And you have somebody tell you, 'But for your dog, my child wouldn't be able to get through this.' This is the best giving back to the community I've ever done."[36]

CHAPTER SEVEN: PRISON DOGS

It could be a scene out of the successful completion of any dog-training program: A group of dogs and humans are paired up, standing in line, waiting to proceed down the aisle to receive a certificate at the graduation ceremony.

The dogs, mostly Labrador retriever mixes, pose jauntily while heeding the occasional gentle command from their trainers to keep their heads still to prevent the blue tasseled graduation caps from falling off.

The women, clad in well-worn jeans and loose-fitting sweatshirts, are grinning a mile wide while trying but ultimately failing to hold back the tears of pride for their own and their dogs' accomplishments after two years of sometimes difficult but ultimately rewarding training, as well as tears of sadness.

For after both humans and canines share in a celebratory graduation cake and ice cream, it'll be the last time they see each other: The dogs will head off to new homes where they'll become guide dogs for the blind, while the women stay behind here in prison where their rooms have bars on the windows and armed guards keep a close eye on the barbed-wire fence along the perimeter.

They've saved each other: The dogs were days — sometimes hours — away from being euthanized at the local shelter or pound, and the women in prison had little to do to keep them from becoming embittered at the thought of spending years or even decades behind bars.

It's safe to say that for many dog lovers, the idea of man's best friend living in prisons is tantamount to abuse and grounds for calling in a report to the humane society. After all, living with criminals behind bars, with the cacophony created by cinder-block walls and the extreme restriction of movement, is not anybody's idea of a good time.

But the truth is that prison programs that train dogs — who are low on the totem pole themselves — for a future life as a service dog or a happy household pet are surprisingly widespread and effective. Both prison officials and assistance-dog experts rave about the effects that these highly disciplined training programs have on both the prisoners and the dogs.

"The inmates are very proud of themselves for having succeeded in a project when most people expected them to fail," says Gloria Gilbert Stoga, who founded Puppies Behind Bars in 1997, one of the first organizations to specifically train guide and service dogs in prisons. "Against the odds, they have undertaken a serious responsibility and stuck with it, sometimes for the first time in their lives. They have done everything they possibly could for almost two years to help a puppy grow into a successful, well-mannered working dog. Above all, they learned what it was to love again, to trust again, and in the words of one of our inmates, 'to be a human being again.'"[1]

This is no surprise to Gennifer Furst, associate professor of sociology and coordinator of the criminal justice program at William Paterson University in New Jersey, and author of *Animal Programs in Prison: A Comprehensive Assessment.* She's been studying such programs for more than a decade and believes their growth will continue; after all, guide- and service-dog programs across the country report they cannot meet the demand for well-trained canines.

"Prison-based dog programs have proliferated not just throughout the United States but around the globe," Furst said. "Particularly since 9/11, the need for working canines has skyrocketed. With service canines, the supply has never been able to keep up with the demand. Now, with wounded veterans returning from the wars in the Middle East with both physical and psychological injuries, there is an even increased demand for service canines. The situation is urgent."[2]

Part of the reason for the proliferation of prison programs is that inmates have the time to devote to the intensive training these highly specialized dogs require. Furst points out that inmates who train dogs are engaging in a form of restitution — this is not merely symbolic busywork as is the case with many prison programs but is very much needed and positively impacts countless people's lives. The inmates who participate in these programs are not only experiencing psycho-social as well as physical benefits, they're also learning vocational skills they can use when they are released. In some programs, inmates can earn a veterinary tech certificate, which will help them find a job when they leave prison. Indeed, many have gone on to work for the shelter or a private prison non-profit once they complete their sentence.

"Prison-based dog programs have no disadvantages," Furst said. "Everyone benefits: society, the inmates, the dogs, and the prison. Dog programs should be in every [prison] in the United States."

Furst researched and published a national survey of prison-based animal programs in the December 2006 issue of *The Prison Journal* and found a variety of programs in use in at least 36 states and 159 facilities. Today, some reports put that figure as being closer to all 50 states and well over 200 prisons.

Gloria Stoga founded Puppies Behind Bars because the demand for guide and service dogs among blind, deaf, and other disabled people far outstripped the available supply of trained dogs. She first became interested in the concept when she read about Dr. Thomas Lane, a retired veterinarian who launched the first puppies-and-prisoners program in 1990 in Gainesville, Florida.

Dr. Lane, in turn, had been inspired by Sister Pauline Quinn, a Dominican nun who started the Prison Pet Partnership Program in Washington State in 1981 specifically to teach inmates how to train dogs who had been abandoned at shelters to assist people who needed a guide or service dog.

But not all the dogs in prison programs are trained specifically to be guide dogs, and not all dogs come from shelters. Puppies Behind

Bars works with a local guide-dog service that provides dogs to the program, while other organizations work specifically on socializing shelter dogs who might otherwise be unadoptable.

For instance, at the Taylor Correctional Institution Work Camp near Perry, Florida, inmates train dogs from the Tallahassee Animal Service Center in an eight-week program called UTOPIA, short for Undergoing Training and Obedience in Prison to Increase Adoptability. After the third year of the program, 162 hard-to-place dogs had graduated, and all were successfully adopted.

"UTOPIA has been successful from the start, because everybody wins," said Department of Corrections secretary Walt McNeil. "The dogs get adopted, the inmates learn a trade, and the owners get a well-trained companion who may have had a very different fate if not for this program."[3]

Warden Duane Spears agreed. "Both staff and inmates love the program," he said. "Inmates take ownership of their assigned dogs and take great pride in their accomplishments." He added that thirty-four of the thirty-six inmates with UTOPIA have been free of disciplinary infractions the last six months.[4]

Still other programs actually have prisoners

train dogs to become bomb- and explosive-detection dogs, while another group — the military — uses imprisoned military offenders at Camp Lejeune Base Brig in North Carolina and the Miramar Consolidated Brig in California to train dogs to become guide and service dogs for the Wounded Warrior Project, serving veterans injured in the line of duty. The Camp Lejeune program works with Carolina Canines for Service; the Miramar inmates work with Canine Companions for Independence.

How It Works

Most prison dog programs follow a similar format: The dogs live with their assigned prisoner 24/7, though in some cases they spend the night in a separate building depending on the degree of security. Programs are held at both minimum- and maximum-security facilities across the country.

The prisoners chosen for the program have usually been incarcerated for at least several years and have had no disciplinary problems in at least the previous six months. Over the course of the program, if an inmate becomes violent or acts out, the dog is immediately taken away and given to another prisoner. Not surprisingly, those in the program usually turn into model prisoners.

At most prisons, a spot in the program is highly coveted, and there's a lengthy waiting list for would-be trainers. Prisoners in the program can become serial trainers — immediately training a new puppy once the previous one graduates — so for many the only way to gain a place on the roster is when a prisoner in the program is released.

In most cases, sex offenders are not allowed to join the program, but those convicted of murder are. Charity Payne is an inmate at the Indiana Women's Prison in Indianapolis. She's serving time for her role as an accomplice in a triple murder, though she was not on the scene when her codefendants committed the crimes. The earliest she can be released from prison is 2078. At her trial, she fully admitted to her role in the murders, which consisted of telling the codefendants where to go to commit what was initially supposed to be a robbery; one defendant was given the death penalty.

It was Payne's honesty that gained her entry into the program, said Sally J. Irvin, executive director of Indiana Canine Assistant & Adolescent Network, who helps prison staff to decide which inmates are allowed to train puppies. "I don't care what you did, I care how much responsibility you take for it," she said. "Charity is an amazing kid. She made some bad choices and takes total responsibility for her choices."[5]

Charity and every other inmate in a prison program essentially gets to spend all day and night with their dogs except for the times when they're at work — though not every inmate in a puppy program has a prison job — or at the cafeteria for meals; some programs allow the puppy raisers to eat in their rooms with their dogs. During these times, the puppy is most often in a crate in the inmate's room or cell. The rest of the time, the inmates are with their dogs, exercising, training, grooming, playing, or attending a class with a professional trainer. However, at some programs, the dogs accompany their inmates everywhere, to work and the cafeteria. And a dog's bathroom breaks usually depend on an inmate's living arrangements and whether they are either on a strict schedule — with guards filling in the gaps when needed — or are able to take the dog out whenever nature calls.

At some programs, including Puppies Behind Bars, two inmates share one dog. One serves as the primary puppy raiser, who is mainly responsible for most of the day-to-day routine, from feeding to training, while the other waits in the wings and is ready to step in in case the first inmate needs a break or has to head out for some reason. Both raisers are required to go to the training sessions led by a professional trainer.

In most cases, all expenses, from veterinary bills to training fees, are borne by the nonprofit organization responsible for placing the dogs after they leave prison, drawing on private donations and fund-raisers; the person who eventually receives the dog may also be required to pitch in with a certain amount. Many inmates use their own money earned from a prison job to buy toys, treats, leashes, and food bowls.

EVERYONE BENEFITS

If there was ever a win-win-win program in prison — or anywhere else, actually — the prison dog programs are a stellar example. Absolutely everyone benefits.

First, the dogs. Those who came into the program from a shelter may have been living in abusive situations or abandoned, and at first it may take a while for them to be able to trust strangers and warm up to them . . . just like the prisoners who train them.

Canine and correctional facility experts assert that dogs in prison programs thrive even in maximum-security institutions, and that it's a much healthier environment than most animal shelters, where they'd be living in a cage or concrete kennel. "Where else are they going to get 24-hour service and hundreds of people to love them?" said Roma Paulson, who manages the prison puppy program at the Mansfield Correctional Institution in Ohio.[6]

Inmates in the program thrive under the responsibility. They are almost certain to become model prisoners because they realize if they act up, they're booted out of the program and their dog is given to another inmate. In addition, life in such a harsh environment can't help but be altered by the dogs' presence. Everyone who comes into contact with them — inmates, staff, visitors — benefits.

"One [inmate] said she had taken almost every group there is to take, from anger management and resiliency to victim impact, but it wasn't until she was in the [dog] program that she got to utilize some of these skills," said Sandy Hand, transition coordinator at the Minnesota Correctional Facility in Shakopee. "They're contributing to the community even while being here."[7]

"These dogs have had such a positive effect on the staff here and all the women," said Marie Clements, an inmate at the Indiana Women's Prison who has trained several dogs for the puppy program. "They've brought life into the prison."[8]

And inmates have gained a newfound respect from not only their fellow inmates but also correctional officers and other staff members, something they may well be unfamiliar with. "[Having] puppies in the prison has made this a different place to work," said Lieutenant Gretta Wilkerson, a correctional officer at Fishkill Correctional Facility in Peekskill, New York. "When you see the dogs walking around you have to smile. It's made us all grow."[9]

Paulson agrees. "It's difficult to walk by a puppy and not smile or reach down for a pat on the head, whether you're a jaded corrections officer or a hardened inmate," she said. "And it's a spark of normalcy [for the inmate]: I can't decide what I eat. I can't decide what I wear. I can't decide where I go. I can't visit with my family, but I can have a dog. And I can have all the love it can give me."[10]

One Mansfield inmate agrees wholeheartedly. "I love dogs," said John W. Smith. "I love the atmosphere of training dogs. People are harder to work with actually than dogs."[11]

Even the trainers gain from interacting with the dogs and prisoners. Elta Woodliff is a dog trainer who runs the puppy program at the Mark H. Luttrell Correctional Center

EDIE

Before she started living at the Mansfield Correctional Institution, Edie was living a hardscrabble life. No one knows how long the mixed-breed dog had fended for herself on the streets of Mansfield, Ohio, scrounging for food and maybe an occasional kind word or pat on the head from a stranger, but it wasn't until she moved behind bars that she received the care and regular feeding that she deserved.

But first she had to get shot.

In her regular wanderings, Edie frequented a couple of different neighborhoods, and many residents grew accustomed to her visits. One didn't, however, and he sent a clear message when he unleashed his twelve-gauge shotgun on the dog. Local animal lovers rescued the dog, paid for her veterinary bills, and then transferred her to the prison, where they knew she would be nursed back to health with the almost constant attention required for her to recover.

Inmate Aaron Gray had been working in the dog-training program at the prison for six months when Edie arrived, and he took full responsibility for the dog, setting his alarm every couple of hours to clean her wounds and give her medicine.

Edie made a full recovery and Gray started to train the little dog who had been close to death when she came to the prison. Even though he had trained other dogs who had moved on to their new owners, Gray took a shine to Edie. He spoke with his family in Cleveland, who agreed to care for the dog when both her recovery and her training were complete.

"It's brought me closer to my family," said Gray. "We have something to talk about."

In the meantime, he steeled himself to continue training as many dogs as possible until his release and reunion with Edie. "This isn't a place to meet friends," he said. "This is a place to do time. [The dogs] are my friends."*

---

*Robert E. Pierre, "Ohio Prisons Go Gladly to the Dogs: Inmates Care for Throwaways and Help Themselves as Well," *Washington Post*, June 3, 2004.

in Memphis. "These people challenge me," she said. "They make me a much better dog trainer."[12]

The people who place the dogs have definitely noticed.

"All the raisers do a good job, but this is a different caliber of dog coming out of the prison program," said Jenine Stanley, the former president of Guide Dog Users, the largest organization of its kind in the world. "They're more stable, more well-adjusted. The one-on-one attention they get as they grow up is really valuable."[13]

"They are extremely well trained," said Deanne Osgood, who adopted a golden retriever from the Mansfield program in 2001. "And they're really socialized after being around other dogs and people all the time."[14]

Jane Russenberger, senior director of breeding and placement for Guiding Eyes for the Blind in Yorktown Heights, New York, agrees. "The love, the level of commitment, the high level of manners the dogs develop, what comes out of the prisons is different from what we're seeing anywhere else," she said.[15]

There are hard numbers to back up the enthusiasm. The Canine Detection Institute at Auburn University in Alabama trains dogs for police and arson-detection programs and used to have future candidates live with puppy-raising families for a year, but they were stymied by the low success rate of the dogs: Only 25 percent of the puppies graduated from CDI. Once the institute began to send puppies to prisons in Florida and

Georgia for basic training, the graduation rate went through the roof, with up to 80 percent of puppies going on to become successful detection dogs. Trainers and CDI staff attribute the increase to exposure to the harsh lights and noises, crowds, and irregular floors in a prison. In other words, puppies raised in prisons were simply desensitized and accustomed to working and staying focused despite a myriad of distractions.

As with other programs that train dogs to become service and guide dogs, despite the high level of success with prison-trained dogs, some are not suited for the life. The Prison Pet Partnership Program estimates that only one out of fifteen to twenty dogs who complete a prison-based program has what it takes to become a service or guide dog; other programs estimate that one-third of dogs go on to successful "careers" as an assistance canine. Happily, all is not lost. For those who don't make it, most graduates of prison programs are quickly adopted in the community or by someone who volunteers with the program.

LETTING GO

Despite the hard work required to train a dog to become a qualified assistance dog, it's never too far from the minds of the inmates that the day will come when all their effort and devotion and love will bring the desired result: The dogs they lived with day and night for up to two years will leave to go live with new owners and do exactly the job they were trained to do.

The dogs "graduate," and depending upon the amount and degree of training may actually be received by their new owners in person. During the time the inmate has been working with the dog, she keeps a journal of sorts, writing down the dog's personality quirks, how to handle the dog, essentially a scrapbook of the time they've spent together. During the ceremony, the inmate hands the leash and book to the new owner, and tears are never far away from all in attendance.

Some programs require dogs and inmates to separate occasionally by having volunteers take the dogs for a weekend as well as on jaunts out in public so they can become accustomed to the very different noise and chaos of nonprison life that includes traffic, strangers, and stores.

"It's especially hard because in many ways [the inmates are] so alone here," said Susan McGhee, head trainer at the Prison Pet Partnership Program in Gig Harbor, Washington. When the feared day finally arrives and the dog leaves, McGhee said that most inmates head for their rooms for the afternoon to be alone. "Most say, 'I'm never doing this again, I can't do this again,' but they always want another dog. Always."[16]

After getting another dog, the prisoners are able to hone their training skills. They also show other inmates who are new to the program the ropes and are better able to anticipate problems that may arise.

Cindy Lee Galvan is an inmate at the Minnesota Correctional Facility in Shakopee and has trained seven dogs in the program there. Despite the difficulty and sadness she faces with every "graduation," she still looks forward to every new dog, not only for herself but also because she hears back from the owners who are thriving because of her work training dogs.

"I guess the story is the same for a lot of us," said Galvan. "You do things that you know are really bad and you don't know how to fix them. And at the time, you don't really care because that's who you are then. Then you grow up and you mature, and you have the opportunity to maybe help somebody else out a little bit. We know that one dog and one program isn't going to do that but that's what we can do right now. That's what we can do today, so that's what we do."

Other inmates in Galvan's program marvel at how working with dogs has so utterly changed them. "Being in prison and being able to give something so honorable, it's an amazing gift," said Heather Ecklund. "To have somebody take that chance on you is an amazing gift also."

"I came in here at 18 and it taught me a lot about responsibility," added Amanda Anderson. "I never realized how much work taking care of a dog was until I was actually doing it. When you're having a bad day, you still have to have a good attitude. It helped me keep going, to grow up in lots of different ways."[17]

Chapter Eight: Medical-Detection Dogs

In the not-so-recent past, when it came to dogs and the world of medicine, well, let's just say that canines were basically considered to be little more than lab rats, used for a variety of experiments, some minor, others not so much.

Happily, this is no longer the case. Today researchers, scientists, and physicians are using dogs in a wide variety of ways, including detecting cancer and heart disease in patients and samples in test tubes, alerting to changes in blood sugar levels among diabetics, and much more. Again, as is the case with many other types of Dogs of Courage, the simple reason behind these trends lies in the canine nose and its ability to detect an almost infinite variety of scents.

How does this work? After all, sniffing out a minute particle of explosives or drugs is a lot different from detecting cancerous cells in a tissue sample, or the ability to notice when a diabetic is about to go into insulin shock or an epileptic is about to experience a seizure.

Or is it? Just as dogs — and other animals — are able to detect the early tremors of an earthquake minutes before it hits, canines who are trained to alert to a variety of medical conditions or to sniff out evidence of malignant cells in a specimen bottle are employing the same canine technology: by sensing minute changes in the norm. They can pick up on the scents in a variety of ways: through breath, test tube samples, urine, feces, or the skin. Cancer cells produce chemicals called volatile organic compounds, which emit distinct odors that dogs — often specifically trained but occasionally not — can pick up on. In many ways, they can sense the storm brewing.

"We are only at the start of working out everything that dogs can detect," said Dr. Claire Guest, the CEO and director of operations of Medical Detection Dogs, a U.K.-based charitable organization that conducts research and training. "It would seem that almost any medical event has an odor change. The clever thing is that the dogs are able to work out what the norm is, and when it changes."[1]

Even though the scientific and medical communities are actively funding and researching the abilities of canines to detect and help defuse medical emergencies before they occur, as well as being able to identify cancers in the lab, the truth is that dog lovers and owners have always been aware that dogs had the ability to serve as medical detectives; they didn't need the medical establishment to tell them what they already knew.

MEDICAL-ALERT DOGS

Medical-detection dogs do more than work in laboratories and sniff out cancers. Some medical-detection dogs are a variation on service dogs and live full-time with individuals with chronic health problems who benefit from having a canine alert them to an imminent problem, such as a seizure or diabetic shock.

Though many service and guide dogs bond closely with their humans, some people believe that medical-alert dogs have to bond even more closely because the dogs have to be trained to notice the slightest change in their owners. For instance, a diabetic-alert dog knows that when he senses a rise in blood sugar, he has to spring into action and do what he was trained to do. And some epileptics experience slight fluttering of their eyelids right before a seizure begins, which can be spotted by a seizure-alert dog long

REMY

Peanut allergies have been on the rise in recent years, and Billy Gensel of Tampa, Florida, falls into the unluckiest category. "If I come in contact with a peanut, or residue of a peanut, then in 15 to 20 seconds I'll be dead," he said.

Merely coming into contact with a seat in a restaurant where someone who ate a handful of peanuts, wiped his hands on his pants, and sat in the spot several days earlier can trigger an attack.

Needless to say, when Remy, a black Lab trained as a peanut-detection dog, came to live with the Gensels, their lives drastically changed, and for the better. Before Remy entered their lives, Billy was essentially confined to his house; any trips to public places were fraught with tension and anxiety, the EpiPen always within quick reach. Now, not only does Remy alert to peanut-contaminated surfaces, but he can also warn Billy and his mom about people in the vicinity who have minute traces of peanut residue on their clothes or hands.

Peanut-detection dogs are still pretty rare, but the Southern Star Ranch Kennel in Florence, Texas, has developed a special program to train these highly skilled canines. In addition to their detection skills, any allergen-detection dog needs a good deal of patience and must be able to tolerate regular baths and cleaning. After all, once Remy finds traces of peanut residue, Billy's mother not only has to wipe down a table and chair in a restaurant with disposable disinfectant wipes but also has to make sure Remy's paws and face are peanut-free.

before a human would be able to pick up on the signs. Though the average time of warning ranges from fifteen to forty-five minutes before a seizure, a few dogs are actually able to detect an impending seizure as much as twelve hours before onset.

In order to become a successful medical-alert dog — sometimes called response dogs — a canine must have some of the characteristics of service and guide dogs, such as an easygoing temperament and a friendly manner when it comes to other people and dogs. Perhaps the most important skill for these dogs is the ability to focus closely on one person, since he is going to have to be able to tune in to minute changes in that person in order to take charge when the need arises. So the ability to ignore distractions like food, other dogs, and noises is vital, especially during the owner's attack.

One immeasurable benefit that medical-alert dogs provide to their owners is the ability to comfort them in stressful times. A number of studies show that the mere presence of an alert dog allows a person to relax and become less anxious. For instance, people who are diabetic or prone to seizures are constantly alert for signs that an attack or spike in blood sugar is near; needless to say, this can ratchet up anxiety levels. However, once they're paired with a suitably trained dog, it's as if the dog has taken up the burden for them, reducing their anxiety while also allowing them plenty of time to prepare for the attack by getting to a safe place and calling for help.

DIABETIC-ALERT DOGS

Diabetes is on the increase throughout the developed world. Whether blood sugar rises or falls, a dog can detect it, thus saving lives.

Paul Jackson has had type 2 diabetes for years and has managed it pretty well on his own. But occasionally he was caught off guard and on the verge of passing out from low blood sugar. One day, his family pointed out that wasn't it funny that just when a hypoglycemic attack was looming — and after it struck — his collie, Tinker, would become extremely anxious.

"He'd lick my face or cry gently while I was sitting down, or bark even," said Jackson. "And then we noticed that this behavior was happening while I was having a hypoglycemic attack, so we just put two and two together."[2]

Indeed, Jackson's experience is not that unusual. Researchers at Queen's University in Belfast in 2009 studied insulin-dependent diabetics who owned dogs. They learned that two of every three diabetics said that their dogs definitely acted agitated and anxious when their blood sugar levels started to plummet. And several diabetics reported that their dogs' unusual behavior actually started before they determined that a hypoglycemic attack was imminent.

Though these dogs are not formally trained, a British organization called Cancer and Bio-Detection Dogs is specifically working to train dogs to become official diabetic-alert dogs. Trainer Kimberly Cox, a diabetic, works with dogs at the center. To her, training a golden retriever named Rory is no different from teaching him to perform tricks or to simply sit or heel.

"I've taught him to recognize the odor, and the odor signals to him a big reward, so he knows to come up to me and recognize that odor," she said.[3]

The odor differs depending upon the blood sugar level's direction: If the level rises, the odor will be somewhat fruity or sugary. If it's heading in the opposite direction, the smell of acetone will emanate from the person.

Dan Warren runs Service Dogs by Warren Retrievers in Orange, Virginia, where he trains diabetic-alert dogs. He was his first client: He learned he had type 1 diabetes in 2004 and realized that a specially trained dog would be the best partner he could have to maintain his health.

"Humans can smell it but it's too late at that point," said Warren. "The dogs are trained to smell it about 45 minutes before the drop or high registers on a meter." He notes that a diabetic-alert dog is particularly useful for alerting to attacks that occur in the middle of the night.[4]

"I haven't slept for more than two hours at a time in the past two-and-a-half years," said Kami Brown of Chesapeake, Virginia, whose six-year-old daughter Marley has spent half her life living with type 1 diabetes. She is on the waiting list for a diabetic-alert dog. "I set my alarm, wake up, give her insulin or candy and go back to bed."[5]

Diabetic-alert dogs are trained not only to respond to a particular smell but also to react if their owner is unresponsive, a common occurrence during a hypoglycemic attack. After his initial alert, a dog will also lick his owner's face. If she still doesn't respond, he will fetch a specially prepared medical kit, bring it to his owner, and then start barking loudly to help wake the person up.

Dogs can do more than just cry or whimper if their diabetic owner is about to become hypoglycemic. A Jack Russell terrier named Kiko in Rockford, Michigan, took drastic measures to get his owner Jerry Douthett's attention: He actually bit off one of his toes!

It wasn't vengeance for too few treats or a lack of attention; it was the dog's way of alerting his master that if he didn't do something about his health — Douthett had type 2 diabetes and didn't know it — Kiko would have to step in.

Douthett had been ignoring an infection on his big toe that had been growing for several months and had shooed Kiko away whenever the dog sniffed at it. He realized something was going on whenever he and his wife, Rosee, visited friends who also had dogs who immediately made a beeline for his toe as well. But he continued to shrug it off, even when his foot swelled to the point that shoes no longer fit and he had to start wearing sandals instead.

One night Douthett partied a little too hard and collapsed into bed when he got home. Though he'd had more margaritas than he could count, he woke up with a start when he realized that Kiko was in the process of chewing off his toe. On the way to the hospital, he cursed out the dog, but when he was admitted with a blood sugar level of 560 — the normal range is between 80 and 120 — he had second thoughts and realized Kiko had essentially saved his life.

"If it hadn't been for that dog, I could have ended up dead," he said. From that day on, Douthett vowed to take better care of his health — including giving up alcohol — and there have been no more infections on his feet. "I don't think Kiko would do it again," he said, "but I wear shoes to bed now."[6]

ALLERGEN-ALERT DOGS

Many people have allergies. But for the vast majority, the worst they have to deal with is a stuffy nose and watery eyes. For the unlucky ones, exposure to even residue of the offending allergen could quickly prove fatal.

Before a Portuguese water dog by the name of Rock'O came into her life, Riley Mers of Monument, Colorado, was afraid to leave the house. It wasn't because the eight-year-old girl was agoraphobic; rather, she had a severe allergy to peanuts, which could potentially kill her. In fact, once when she was at the playground, a tiny fragment of a peanut shell got through her sandal, and the resulting burn was so severe that she had to go to the emergency room.

But with Rock'O by her side, always alert to the presence of peanut residue that may be invisible to the naked eye, the little girl is able to lead a life that comes pretty close to those of her schoolmates and friends. "It's just so life-changing you wouldn't believe it," she said, referring to the dog as her guardian angel.

She is able to go to a few classes each week at a local elementary school, though to keep the risk of peanut exposure low, she also takes several courses online in the safety of her home. Even though the school principal has ordered that the school cafeteria refrain from serving peanut butter to students, there's always the chance that a classmate will bring a peanut butter sandwich from home, so it's safest for Riley to keep her school attendance to a minimum.

Bill Whitstine, a master trainer with Florida Canine Academy, taught Rock'O, who was his first peanut-detection dog; previously, he had trained dogs to alert to everything from bedbugs to bombs and drugs. "This really is a bomb dog for this child, because the peanut is a bomb for her," he said. Brett Mers, Riley's father, says that Rock'O provides "long-range radar."[7]

Sharon Perry of the Southern Star Ranch Boarding Kennel, in Florence, Texas, runs Peanut Detection Dogs, and she believes that it is just as important for an allergen-alert dog to be properly trained as one who searches for bombs. "It has to be done right, because somebody's life depends on this dog," she said. "If these dogs miss a peanut, the child is dead."[8]

SEIZURE-ALERT DOGS

When it came to caring for Colin, her eleven-year-old son, Candace Walker of Grayslake, Illinois, doesn't know how she managed before Donut, a golden retriever seizure-alert dog, entered her family's lives. Colin has Dravet syndrome, a rare form of childhood epilepsy, and Candace was constantly preoccupied with the possibility of a seizure as well as her son's habit of wandering off when the family was out shopping. It's important for Colin to receive his medication as quickly as possible in order to reduce the severity of a seizure.

BOO

Pam Minicucci of North Haven, Connecticut, sees to it that her seven-year-old daughter, Gianna, doesn't take a step without Boo, her peanut-detection Saint Bernard. "The dog is just one way we can help our daughter have a more normal life," she said. "Our goal is for the dog to be with her everywhere she goes. I don't expect people to change their world for us, but I do expect them to allow us to protect our child in the way we need to."*

Those dangers can be well hidden and go well beyond finding peanut traces on a nearby stranger's jeans. One day, the three were shopping in a big-box store, and Boo refused to let Gianna and her mom head down an aisle stocked with paper products. Pam surveyed the shelves and saw nary a peanut-butter jar or cookie in sight, so she thought the dog was giving a false alert.

She told Gianna to go ahead, but again Boo blocked access to the aisle. Pam took a closer look and got down on her hands and knees. Sure enough, tucked under the shelf on the floor was a mousetrap stuffed with peanut butter as bait.

*Brian Newsome, "Peanut-Sniffing Dog Is Allergic Girl's Best Friend," *Colorado Springs Gazette,* February 17, 2009.

"Colin had been 'Code Adam' [a missing child] more times than I can count," said Walker. "Now Donut is tethered to him when we go out, so he doesn't wander away anymore. Plus, Donut has a harness that carries his seizure medicine."[9]

Like other medical-detection dogs, canines who are trained to alert their owners or call for help in the event of a seizure caused by epilepsy or another health condition sense a change in their owner's blood chemistry. Because most seizures result in a loss of consciousness, it's also important for a seizure-alert dog to be able to alert to an oncoming seizure and then take action in a number of ways before the person can hurt himself or others. Some seizure-alert dogs paw a person's leg or arm, others bark, while still other dogs actually lightly nip a hand or ankle.

"Donut is trained to alert us by barking," said Walker. "Typically he 'woofs' right before one, but one time he warned us 45 minutes in advance. Donut will also lie down next to Colin during a seizure. I think he can pick up the scent of the seizure in advance."[10]

Theories differ as to how seizure-alert dogs know when an episode is imminent. "Right now, it's only a theory that these dogs can smell a seizure in advance," said Garett Auriemma, a former spokesperson with the Epilepsy Foundation of Greater Chicago. "What we think [happens] is these dogs form a strong bond with the owner and learn to recognize signs or things people do before they have a seizure. So the dog may say, 'Oh, that usually leads to the thing I need to do, like bark.' It's very rare for a dog to predict a seizure without knowing you first."[11]

A seizure-alert dog may also climb on top of a person, preventing him from wandering off and helping to keep him safe. Another technique is for the dog to essentially herd the human, keeping her sequestered and safe in one spot in order to prevent injury and also keeping other people at a distance. Dogs can also be trained to call 911 for help through a special communication device: As soon as their paw hits the button, emergency services are alerted and help is on the way.

For those who suffer from seizures, particularly children, a seizure-alert dog can assume some of the characteristics of a service-dog relationship. For instance, if a child has to wear a helmet to school, he'll probably have to deal with other kids teasing or even bullying him. But if there's a dog constantly by his side, not only does this serve as a deterrent to abusive behavior, but it can actually open up the possibility of new friendships, which means the child feels less isolated and alone. In addition, the medication that these kids take may have unwelcome side effects, such as loss of balance and aggressive behavior toward others. In this case, a dog can be trained to watch for these changes in behavior and intervene by helping to upright the child and/or by serving as a distraction.

OTHER MEDICAL CONDITIONS

Trained detection dogs are becoming so accepted as a means of helping people with chronic health conditions to stay safe that it's anyone's guess as to what they'll be trained to detect in the future. Although Jim Touzeau's Australian cattle dog, Teka, wasn't specially trained to know when her owner was having a massive heart attack at their home in Queensland, Australia, the dog nevertheless sprang into action in 2007, and she knew exactly what to do.

Touzeau was lying on the ground when

Teka found him. The dog started barking and jumping on his chest, seemingly performing a canine version of CPR. Amazingly enough, it worked. Between the motion and the barking, Touzeau came to long enough to call for help.

"I don't know if she actually kick-started my heart, but she was really thumping my chest with her two front feet. The doctors said that if I hadn't come to and called for help, chances are I would be dead," he said. "My heart had definitely stopped."

Touzeau had brought Teka home three years earlier after his wife died. "Teka's a terrific companion," he said. "She just never leaves my side. Because it's just the two of us, I rely on her and she relies on me."

Still, it was the first time the dog had reacted in that fashion. "It was out-of-the-blue [behavior] for her," Touzeau continued. "She must have been thinking, 'I better wake this fella up or I won't get any dinner.' "[12]

For saving Touzeau's life, the RSPCA awarded Teka a Purple Cross for bravery in a special ceremony. And though he had no doubt that Teka would do the very same thing in the future, Touzeau wasn't taking any chances.

After the ceremony, he had a cardiac defibrillator implanted in his chest.

Theo, a cocker spaniel in Essex, England, also wakes up her owner, but she is trained to do it and sometimes is called on to perform the task several times a day.

Kelly Sears, Theo's owner, has narcolepsy, a condition where she can fall asleep without warning, which can obviously put her into dangerous situations, from collapsing on the street to passing out on the bus. Now, whenever Sears falls asleep, Theo knows to lick her face to help her regain consciousness.

"Theo has made a huge difference to my life. I go out on my own with him and feel confident," she said. "I fall asleep anywhere — shopping, on the bus and I've fallen downstairs a few times. People often call an ambulance, but because Theo wears a jacket saying 'medical alert dog in training' they're not so worried."[13]

CANCER-DETECTION DOGS

Maureen Burns of Rugby, England, knew something was up when her collie mix, Max, started to act depressed. Max was typically a happy-go-lucky dog, up for anything as long as it involved spending time with Maureen, but in the spring of 2008, the dog started to act sad. Regardless of what Burns did to encourage her dog, Max just moped around and appeared to have little energy.

Though Burns was concerned, she felt there was little she could do and expected that in time the dog's depression would lift. One day during this period, Max did something he had never done before: He spent a lengthy amount of time sniffing at Maureen's mouth and then nudged her right breast. Then he repeated himself: first smelling her mouth before moving on to her breast, always in the same spot.

In 1998, Burns had had a breast cancer scare with a lump removed that was benign, and she had adhered to a strict schedule of self-exams every month since her surgery. After Max performed his curious stunt, she decided to do her monthly self-exam. The dog watched while she did the procedure.

Indeed, she did find a lump, which she thought was again benign since her most recent mammogram had come back clean. But just as she felt it more closely, she glanced at Max, who was watching her every move. "Our eyes met and I just remember he looked so sad," said Burns. "I knew in that instant that something was badly wrong."

She called for an appointment with her doctor, who confirmed her suspicion. "When the nurse told me I had breast cancer, my first response was, 'I know, my dog told me!'" said Burns. "I expected her to laugh but instead she told me she had heard of similar cases."

Surgery was scheduled, and the cancer was removed. The moment Burns arrived back from the hospital, Max welcomed her home. "He was acting like he was a puppy again," she said. "It was as though he knew I was okay again. He stopped sniffing me and became very playful. I owe him so much."[14]

Indeed, some dogs are being trained to detect cancers; however, unlike diabetic- and seizure-alert dogs, these cancer-detection dogs do not typically work with individual patients. Instead, they are trained as a kind of hyperacute lab sensor. Dr. Claire Guest says that her first intimation that dogs have the natural ability to identify cancer and other diseases came after she heard about a woman whose dalmatian wouldn't stop sniffing and licking a mole on the woman's leg.

"Although [the doctor] thought it was harmless, he removed it," said Guest. As it turned out, the woman had malignant melanoma. "We believe that each disease has its own scent signature and if we could isolate that, routine screening would speed up diagnosis." She also noted that specially trained dogs provide a method of early detection that often eludes humans, and many times, when a person finally decides to see a doctor and is diagnosed, the cancer has advanced to a terminal state.[15]

Since her revelation, Dr. Guest has trained a number of cancer-detection dogs, including Tangle, a cocker spaniel who can detect evidence of bladder cancer in urine samples. Guest once trained guide dogs for deaf individuals, but the promise of cancer detection is so great — and medical researchers were so intent on gaining access to these dogs — that she switched tracks from training dogs to turn on light switches and open doors to teaching them to seek out the sample with a life-threatening cancerous growth.

One thorny issue that developed for the dogs in one study concerned their inability, like many humans, not to take their work home with them. For instance, these dogs work part time, and the rest of the time they're like any other dog, living with a family, romping through fields on a chase, and sniffing curiously at other humans, some of whom undoubtedly have undiagnosed cases of cancer.

A yellow Lab named Kobe was trained in cancer detection at the Pine Street Foundation in Anselmo, California, one of the first clinics to train dogs in the field. Maria Rios,

Kobe's owner, had her first inkling of how effectively the dog had been trained when she visited an aunt who had been recently diagnosed with ovarian cancer.

"Kobe had been around her prior to her having cancer but he never reacted strangely," said Rios. From the moment they arrived at her house, the dog instantly reacted. "He just went absolutely crazy, barking at her. I had never seen him behave that way. He barked at her even when she went behind a closed door. I didn't put two and two together until she suddenly passed away three weeks later. We knew she had cancer, but we had no idea that she was going to pass away so soon."

Kobe also alerted on people while at the local dog park, which Rios said provided her with some uncomfortable decisions to make. "A handful of times, he'd zoom in on a person and behave the way he did with my aunt. It was very difficult for us because this was prior to [the study] being published and we didn't know if we should scare these people because we didn't know [the results].

"I have heard of an example where another dog identified someone positively and it's possible to say they saved that person's life," Rios continued. "Difficult as it may seem, it may not be a bad idea to bring it up in a non-urgent manner. To just say, 'This is what the dog has been trained to do and I don't want to worry you, but you might want to get checked for the specific kind of cancer this dog has been trained to detect.' You could also let them know that it's not 100 percent."[16]

Claire Guest says these are exciting times to be in this research field. "Now that we know that dogs are able to detect human disease by its odor, and that different diseases have different odors, the potential is just incredible to help individuals with life-threatening conditions but also to have new ways of looking at diagnosis of life-threatening diseases such as cancer."[17]

CHAPTER NINE:
WILDLIFE-DETECTION
AND -CONSERVATION DOGS

North of the Arctic Circle, the ecosystem consists not just of polar bears but also of thousands of living things. Although recent research into global warming has largely focused on shorter winters and melting glaciers and on how the polar bears are coping and adapting — or not — scientists know there is an entire hidden ecosystem that lies ten feet or more under the ice as well as miles away in crevices and knolls throughout the frozen tundra. Needless to say, reaching these places is an incredible challenge, but finding and studying the rich diversity of creatures could help reveal valuable clues that could eventually lead to implementing a concrete solution.

Enter the ecodog, or wildlife-detection dog, a special courageous canine trained to locate everything from pollutants in water to the presence of endangered birds and sea turtles, and even common everyday "wildlife" found in virtually every home in America. Researchers already realize that there's no beating a dog's nose when it comes to helping them do their jobs better, and so many scientists are increasing their use of ecodogs in their work.

While polar bears are listed as threatened under the Endangered Species Act of 1973, garnering more attention and research funding for other less well-known Arctic species is difficult and ultimately depends on first locating and then counting the wide variety of birds, animals, and fish that may be affected by warmer temperatures, and then tracking their numbers from one year to the next.

Finding ringed seals is the job of Brendan Kelly, an associate professor of marine biology at the University of Alaska Southeast in Juneau, who has conducted research in the Arctic for three decades. He's trained several black Labs, including one named Cooper, to detect ringed seals from almost two miles away. And this one species of seal is just the tip of the iceberg, so to speak. "There is an elaborate ecosystem [under the ice]," says Kelly. "Only with the use of that nose on the Labradors can we go out and find out that that barren-looking icescape is in fact loaded with mammals."[1]

Whether they're working in the Arctic Circle to find seals or along the equator in Mexico to sniff out sea turtle nesting spots, dogs who can track wildlife of all kinds are increasing in numbers as well as in scope, and in some surprising places.

"Wildlife detection dogs have been mostly used in airports to detect contraband, including endangered species and wildlife products, but in recent years interest has grown in using the dogs to help scientists track biological targets in natural settings," said Sarah Reed, a postdoctoral fellow at Colorado State University's Department of Fish, Wildlife, and Conservation Biology. "Working with dogs can greatly improve our ability to detect rare species and help us to understand how these species are responding to large-scale environmental changes, such as habitat loss and fragmentation."[2]

As is the case with other Dogs of Courage, not every canine is cut out for this kind of work. "The dogs that do really well in this type of work are high energy, which also makes them hard to live with as pets," said Aimee Hurt, cofounder of Working Dogs for Conservation, a Montana-based group. "Those are often the types of dogs that end up in shelters. They are not kennel dogs. They need a job."[3]

Even then, the odds aren't good. Because of the skills that these dogs must have in order to do their jobs, Hurt estimates that just one of two hundred to three hundred dogs considered for wildlife-detection work has what it takes to start training, and less than half of those go on to full-time employment. But those who do make the cut go on to perform extremely valuable work.

THE POOP

One of the talents that make wildlife-detection dogs extremely valuable is precisely what dog owners frown upon: They're extraordinarily good at finding scat, or animal feces, of all types.

"Once the ability to extract and analyze DNA improved, researchers recognized the value of scat as a way to non-invasively monitor the location and population size of key species," said Hurt. "With scat, you can confirm the ID of species and even individuals, as well as analyze hormone levels and diet. It's a very valuable data deposit. So then it became a matter of finding ways to better track the scat, and dogs naturally came to mind."[4]

Scientists also analyze scat for the presence of poisons and toxins, stress and hormonal levels, and diet.

"We wanted to record how far away dogs

can detect the scat, and to determine how that is influenced by factors in the environment, such as wind direction, humidity and temperature," Reed added. "One of the things we're trying to do is help design tests and create metrics that could be used to evaluate dogs as part of a certification program."[5]

Scat-sniffing dogs provide another big bonus: "We [can] track both trap-loving and trap-shy animals," said Samuel Wasser, a biologist at the University of Washington's Center for Conservation Biology. "Male bears are more willing to take risks than females, especially those with cubs. Dogs find scat from all target animals. Plus, some species are masters at eluding the notice of humans, even if they're hiding in plain sight."[6]

But dogs can do more than just sniff for poop on land. Amazingly enough, dogs are being trained to work on the water, checking for scat from a dwindling population of orcas, or killer whales, in Puget Sound.

"We were losing animals and we don't exactly understand why," said Brad Hanson, a wildlife biologist with the National Oceanic and Atmospheric Administration Fisheries Service.[7] Some theories focus on less available food — salmon — in the Pacific Northwest, while others suggest that water pollution and an overload of underwater noise from an increase in oceanic traffic are possible culprits.

To find out, University of Washington researchers got out on the water and collected scat from the orcas. They had a little help from a black Lab named Tucker who already had two strikes against him: In his young life he had been through two homes. Plus, he had failed to pass the tests to become a police dog.

But Tucker had yet another strike against him that made Heath Smith, the director of the orca scat project, take notice, one that is highly unusual for a Lab: The dog was afraid of getting wet.

In Smith's eyes, that was a perfect characteristic. If he *did* love the water, then that meant he'd be constantly jumping in during the research. Smith and his colleagues wanted a dog who would jump in *only* when he detected orca poop.

"We wanted a dog that was not so focused on getting in the water," he said. "He still doesn't like it at all. If he does jump overboard we know there's scat in the water. We haven't had a dog that has caught on quicker. He just knew this was what he wanted to do."[8]

There's one more scat- and water-detection dog to mention. Sable is a German shepherd mix who lives in Lansing, Michigan, with his owner and trainer, Scott Reynolds, an employee with Tetra Tech, an environmental-engineering firm that, among other things, helps detect water contamination. One standard project is to pinpoint the exact location that raw sewage and pollutants enter municipal sewer systems. Traditional methods include tracking water flow via a dye test, where technicians flush dye into a toilet and then track where it goes. The process is time-consuming and also not fail-safe, plus it requires chemical tests to make a positive confirmation.

Sable's sniffing skills have made water pollution experts sit up and take notice: Results reveal that the dog's success rate was close to 90 percent. Plus, the results come a *lot* faster.

"Instead of sending a sample to a lab and finding out two weeks or two months later and having to go back and take three or four or five more samples, you can narrow it down and eliminate some of the tests you have to take," said Sue Kubic, a senior engineer with Michigan's Genesee County Drain Commission. "We can take it from [testing] 200 houses to maybe we only need to do dyed-water testing for 10," Reynolds said.[9]

Some wildlife does more harm than good when it comes to the environment.

Burmese pythons in Florida's Everglades, for instance. They're extremely invasive, preying on native wildlife like birds and mammals; they've also been known to attack dogs and cats in suburban neighborhoods, as well as the occasional human. They entered the wild when owners released them after they grew larger than expected and have become an increasing problem in Florida in the last several decades. In addition, in 1992, Hurricane Andrew damaged a warehouse where many were stored, which released even more. Researchers from Auburn University's School of Forestry and Wildlife Sciences in Alabama brought Jake and Ivy, both black Labrador retrievers, to Everglades National Park to help find the pythons.

"Pythons are very cryptic," said Christina Romagosa, a research fellow at Auburn. "Their pattern camouflages them very well in the grasses and things the snakes are found in. People are quite limited because we can't see them. But the dogs will use their sense of smell to find the snakes.[10]

"We found the use of detection dogs to be a valuable addition to the current tools used to manage and control pythons," said Romagosa. "Dog search teams can cover more distance and can have higher accuracy rates in particular scenarios than human searchers. We suggest that dogs be used as a complement to current search and trapping methods." On one recent visit, Jake and Ivy helped find nineteen pythons between six and eight feet long, including one pregnant snake. Romagosa and her colleagues schedule searches in the Everglades mostly in winter to prevent overheating the canine members of their team, not to mention that dogs can search for longer stretches in less humid weather.[11]

Wildlife doesn't have to be mobile to be destructive. In the western United States, for instance, spotted knapweed is a quickly spreading nonnative invasive plant that draws more water from the ground than native noninvasive vegetation. Plus, its spiny exterior can damage the digestive systems of animals that consume it. For that reason alone, cattle and other livestock ranchers have a keen interest in eradicating the weed from their land.

Kim Goodwin, invasive weed prevention coordinator at Montana State University in Bozeman, conducted a study to determine if dogs could be trained to find the plant faster than humans. Detection dogs used in airports, post offices, and cargo ships served as her inspiration.

"I thought maybe dogs could do the same thing across a landscape," she said. "And to be most effective with [detecting] weeds spreading, we have to [catch] them early."[12]

Her experiment indeed proved that her theory was viable. She put the skills of three dogs — a mixed-breed shepherd named Nightmare and two German shepherds named Tsavo and Rio — up against twelve humans. Both sides surveyed a meadow for the invasive plant over the course of several trials, first when the weed was sparsely dispersed and then when it was densely populated. In both cases, the dogs came out ahead, locating the weed 81 percent of the time, while the humans' success rate was only 59 percent. The dogs were also better than humans when it came to finding small plants.

To complete the picture, dogs are also actively employed to find bugs and insects that can damage plants. In Massachusetts, the U.S. Department of Agriculture's Animal and Plant Health Inspection Service used trained dogs to detect the Asian long-horned beetle throughout the state.

The invasive beetles can cause extensive damage, from weakening a tree's basic structure to introducing a fungus. If the infestation is severe enough, the tree may die. Using a combination of detection dogs and other methods, the USDA surveyed more than 1.5 million trees in Worcester County and after positively identifying an infested tree, they used a variety of methods to eliminate the beetles, including quarantine, insecticide, and destruction. As a result, the agency reported a 90 percent drop in the number of infested trees in the county over three years.

On the other side of the country, in the California wine region, dogs sniff out mealybugs, which are a real problem in vineyards; if left untreated, they can devastate a crop and wipe out an entire vintage. They run roughshod over a crop, affecting the vine, leaves, and fruit, where they excrete a sugary substance that often creates mold and disease. The invasive bug first showed up in large numbers in the 1990s, but it developed serious traction in the region as it rapidly spread throughout the 2000s, motivating grape growers to seek effective solutions.

They knew they needed to take drastic measures, since by the time a human spots a mealybug — which ranges in size from 1/20th to 1/5th of an inch — it's pretty much too late and the damage has already been done. A dog is able to catch the infestation in the early stages, when an affected vine can be treated with insecticide or removed in order to prevent spread to neighboring vines. If the infestation spreads, not only throughout one vineyard but to neighboring ones as well, the only option, other than pulling up all the vines, is to spray the entire vineyard, which releases more chemicals into the ground at a much higher cost, economically and environmentally.

"As a grower, you can't be asleep at the wheel with this pest," said Sonoma County viticulture adviser Rhonda Smith of the University of California Cooperative Extension. "The bottom line is that an infestation leaves the fruit unmarketable."[13]

Katey Taylor, a viticulturist at Domaine Chandon in Napa Valley, teamed up with several other winemakers in 2006, when the infestation threat was at its highest, to raise $33,000 to fund a study in collaboration with the Assistance Dog Institute in Santa Rosa to see if dogs could detect mealybug infestation in its earliest stages. The study's results were positive, and numerous winemakers acquired trained dogs for use in their own vineyards.

At Honig Vineyard and Winery in Rutherford, dogs were able to detect mealybug pheromones, which then allowed vineyard workers to treat the affected vines. "It worked quite well," said owner Michael Honig, though he admitted that it was necessary to limit the time and area that the dogs spent on mealybug patrol since their success rates declined after a couple of hours. "They get tired if you try to cover hundreds of acres."[14]

In fact, the dogs were so successful that, at least in Honig's vineyards, the dog patrol is no longer necessary.

FINDING ENDANGERED SPECIES AND PLANTS

Wildlife-detection dogs are equally skilled at finding noninvasive animals and plants that are endangered. One example is the Kemp's ridley, considered to be the sea turtle that is in the most danger of becoming extinct.

Rancho Nuevo, a secluded Mexican beach about two hundred miles from Brownsville, Texas, is the only known region in the world where the turtle creates its nests and hatches its babies. In the 1980s, only 250 females were known to exist, and researchers and conservationists were worried that any kind of natural or man-made disaster — from a hurricane to an oil spill — would decimate the already fragile numbers.

American sea turtle researchers helped establish another nesting beach on San Padre Island in Texas during that time, by flying in several thousand turtle eggs each year to help give the virtually extinct species another chance. Researchers and volunteers helped out during nesting season by locating nests of eggs and removing those they found to incubators inside the Sea Turtle Science and Recovery program on the island, which is part of the National Park Service.

The problem was that no matter how quickly the volunteers located the eggs, they couldn't locate all the nests. And the future of the Kemp's ridley was far from secure; though good progress had been made — researchers found ninety-three nests in 2008, up from just five in 2000 — they estimated that approximately two thousand nests were needed to bring the turtle out of the endangered category.

Enter Ridley, a Texas terrier owned by Donna Shaver, director at the sea turtle program, who drew on the less savory traits of terriers to help preserve the species. "I've known for years that dogs and coyotes are two of the prime predators of wild turtle nests in many nations, especially in Central America," said Shaver. "So I was anxious to see if Ridley could find the 'missing' nests."

Ridley was "hired" in 2008, and after an initial intensive training session, he was

TWISTER

Green is good when it comes to creating energy, but the growth of wind farms in Continental Europe and the United Kingdom has had a negative effect on one species of animal that is protected in the region: bats.

When the wind farms took root on the Continent several decades ago, conservationists started to notice a rapid drop in the local bat population wherever the giant turbines were erected. When the tiny bodies were found in the underbrush, they were pretty much intact, so researchers knew the increase in deaths wasn't caused by

Photo: Mike Dean of Eye Imagery

collisions with the massive blades of the wind-generated energy sources. In time, they discovered that they were dying off because of the rapid change in air pressure around the turbines, which their bodies are not built to withstand.

"It's very similar to the bends, which happens to divers when they come up to the surface too fast," said Louise Wilson, head trainer at Wagtail International, a company that trains dogs in several areas of detection, from explosives to drugs. "Bats don't have rigid lungs as birds do, so they can't cope with the sudden changes in air pressure. Their lungs literally explode."

The first step was to gain an accurate count of the numbers of bats that were dying. "They're so tiny that when they are dead, they just look like leaves on the floor," said Wilson.

That's where a springer spaniel by the name of Twister comes in, who works alongside Wilson. "Dogs can find these tiny bodies by scent, where humans would just walk straight past them buried in thick grass or undergrowth. Training [Twister] made us realize just how difficult it is to see these bats. Often the handler still won't see them, so we have trained the dogs to actually indicate more closely by putting their nose right on the bat."*

After Wilson and Twister are called to a scene to survey the bat carnage, they plug the numbers into a formula developed by Bio3, a Portuguese company, which can then inform the wind farm company about the actual numbers so they can take steps to reduce the mortalities; one possible solution is to reduce the speed of the blades on days when wind speeds are low. Bats don't normally fly when conditions are windy.

"Using properly trained dogs is much less invasive and much cheaper than using people, it's also much quicker and provides more accurate figures and that's important for wind farm companies and civil engineering firms or for conservation groups," Wilson noted.[†]

---

*Mark Dowling, "Dogs Sniff Out a Solution to Wind Farm Bat Death," *Chester Chronicle* (U.K.), November 18, 2010.

[†]Kate Forrester, "Meet Twister, the Bat-Hunting Dog Detective: Now He's Got a 'Green' Mission in Portugal," *Liverpool Daily Post,* May 30, 2011.

brought on board. Now during nesting season, after volunteers have combed the beach, Ridley takes over. Unlike his untrained counterparts who attack the eggs in a frenzy, Ridley knows to tread more lightly in order to preserve the eggs.

"I actually think Ridley understands just how important what he's doing is; he gets so excited when he finds a nest, even before he gets his reward," said Shaver.[15]

Conservation dogs are also being trained to catch people stealing rare plants and flowers from public lands and roadsides, whether it's for personal use or for sale on a wholesale or retail basis. In North Carolina in the early 2000s, public lands were under siege, as approximately $5.3 million in valuable ginseng root was taken illegally just in the Great Smoky Mountains National Park.

"[We can] attribute it to higher prices charged in the marketplace, the numbers of unusual plants desired by collectors, their medicinal uses and the money some of these wild stocks bring," said Jim Corbin, a plant protection specialist with the North Carolina Department of Agriculture. The department brought in some canine reinforcements to help catch the bad guys in an innovative program where thousands of ginseng plants were injected with an orange dye, which would accomplish two things: It would make the product less valuable and palatable to many customers, and it would mark the sellers as dealing in illegally obtained agriculture.[16]

A specially trained dog — who detects only the dyed ginseng root, not the real thing — helped out in cases where the procurement was less clear, and his efforts resulted in nine captures of illegal ginseng.

INDOORS: FROM TERMITES TO MOLD

Dogs can be just as effective when it comes to searching for wildlife inside the home. There are any number of professionals who claim that they'll help eliminate many different kinds of pests from a household — spraying poison and setting traps are just two of many tools in their arsenal that may or may not work. To increase their success rate, not to mention the satisfaction of their customers, many are starting to bring a canine employee or two onto the payroll since a dog's good sense of smell can work wonders in finding a wide variety of unwanted household intruders.

Dogs can also help prevent the problem from recurring. After all, once the insects and/or mold are located, treatment is easy, but in many cases it just deals with the surface problem and not the cause, such as an insidious water drip or hidden termite nest. Many an unsuspecting homeowner has discovered that unless you find — and eliminate — the actual source of the problem, the pests are bound to return time and time again.

This is where canine helpers excel over their human counterparts: They don't discriminate. To them, mold is mold and termites are termites. They find everything, from the damage that is obvious to the eye to the often buried root.

No matter what they're searching for, the method is the same. The dog locates the source and then the humans take over and do their thing, whether it's removing the source of infestation and/or treating it with chemicals and insecticides. And the canine teams are usually called in after other, more traditional solutions have failed.

Termite inspector Rick Wade is a convert. It helps too that Wade is also a dog trainer by trade. Based in Raleigh, North Carolina, he works alongside Silas, a black Lab–terrier mix.

"The dogs can find them where we can't," he said. "We're only looking for them, but the dogs are smelling them."[17]

And as with plenty of other canine-detection models, dogs are a lot faster than humans. "We can go through a room in about two minutes with better than 90 percent accuracy, which is nearly impossible to do with a visual human inspector," said Doug Summers of the Florida Canine Academy, who trains pest-control experts and dogs to work as a team.[18]

One of the most well-publicized ways that dogs have been used in the last few years is detecting bedbugs. With a nationwide epidemic of bedbug infestation — and with the pests ranging in size from 1 to 7 millimeters long they're pretty difficult for humans to see — the search for a solution to first detect and then permanently eradicate these pests has kept specially trained dogs and their handlers quite busy.

In fact, with reported cases of bedbug infestation in New York City jumping from 537 in 2004 to almost 13,000 in 2010, having dogs search for bedbugs has become a big business. David Latimer runs Forensic and Scientific Investigations, a canine scent-detection company in Alabama, and reports that the increase in this part of his business "has been the most dramatic of any canine scent detection since bomb dogs after 9/11."[19]

The National Pest Management Association is even getting in on the trend, holding regular conferences to offer certification to qualified canine and handler teams.

"The bedbug training is sort of like hitting the Lotto," said José "Pepe" Peruyero, a handler and trainer at J&K Canine Academy in High Springs, Florida. "Everybody's interested now."[20]

Though many dog owners are curious about cashing in on the demand — especially since many bedbug dog-and-handler teams charge up to $300 an hour for their services in some parts of the country — bedbug-sniffing dogs are like any other working dogs: They have to have a high toy or food drive and be able to tune everything else out in the sheer pursuit of the bug.

"You want to make sure they're taught what to look for, and if they find a missing pb-and-j sandwich under a couch cushion that they're not going to be rewarded," said Missy Henriksen, vice president of public affairs for the National Pest Management Association.[21]

Unlike bedbugs or termites, both of which have a scent that is impossible for a human to pick up, you're able to smell mold when it becomes overwhelming, and of course the telltale dark stain on a wall or ceiling is a dead giveaway.

But what about mold that is hidden and not developed yet to the point where a mere human realizes that it's there?

Again, dogs excel. And while mold that's visible is relatively easy to treat and clean, locating the exact root of the source can be a real headache. But not for a properly trained mold-detection dog, who can pinpoint the precise spot of an unknown drip in an inner wall, making it possible to treat and eliminate the mold without destroying walls and ceilings, which is what most humans need to do in order to even detect the problem.

Sometimes even severe cases of mold are invisible and odorless. And it's always best to catch the problem before it reaches the point where not only your house is threatened but also your health. "Mold that goes on undetected will continue to grow and you can end up with multiple health issues," said Larry Hite of Tracy, California, a home inspector and arson investigator who works with a Jack Russell terrier named Abby. "Some examples of this can be headache, fatigue, nose bleeds, chronic cough or cold, and neurological disorders. Having a mold detection dog can be instrumental in helping us find the mold, so we can get the job done quickly and efficiently."[22]

And a dog can come in handy when members of a household are already having health issues but are stymied as to the cause. Mike and Melenda Lanius, who run MoldBlasters, regularly call on their black giant schnauzer Ebony for help in tough cases. In one home inspection, the dog showed unusual interest in the forced hot-air furnace. Mike Lanius looked all around it but found nothing. When Ebony persisted, Lanius decided to take the furnace apart. As soon as he opened the filter, he realized why the dog had alerted. The filter was filled with mold. "Mold on the filter means it is being circulated throughout the whole house," said Lanius.[23]

In addition to detecting unwanted "wildlife" inside the home, canines are skilled at sniffing out pests in commercial establishments like retail stores, restaurants, and hospitals. In fact, some trained dogs are increasingly being hired to detect a particular type of critter that may have their feline counterparts yowling in protest.

"People know the mice are there because they can see the droppings, but they don't always know where to place traps," said Colin Singer, managing director at Wagtail International, a detection dog company in north Wales in the U.K. "Dogs can tell their handlers where the mice are coming in and out, and hence the best place for catching them."[24]

CHAPTER TEN:
CIVILIAN DOGS

All Debbie Parkhurst of Calvert, Maryland, wanted was an afternoon snack.

What she got instead was a close brush with death, while Toby, her golden retriever, won the title of Dog of the Year 2007, awarded by the ASPCA.

One day in March 2007, Parkhurst grabbed an apple to take an afternoon break from her at-home work as a jewelry designer, something she had done thousands of times before, but this time something went wrong. A chunk of fruit got stuck in her throat, blocking her windpipe. She tried to dislodge it by using the Heimlich maneuver on herself, but the apple remained stuck.

Toby had been relaxing nearby, but when he saw his owner in distress, he quickly took action to help her. "The next thing I know, Toby's up on his hind feet and he's got his front paws on my shoulders," said Parkhurst. "He pushed me to the ground, and once I was on my back, he began jumping up and down on my chest."

The piece of apple shifted and she took a deep breath. Then Toby proceeded to lick her face to keep her conscious until help could arrive.

"Normally I peel them, but I read in *Good Housekeeping* magazine that the skin has all the nutrients, so I ate the skin, and that's what caused me to choke," she said.[1]

"I literally had pawprint-shaped bruises on my chest. The doctor said I probably wouldn't be here without Toby."[2]

Two things are for sure: Parkhurst will never stop feeling grateful to Toby, and if she ever chooses to eat an unpeeled apple, she'll make sure that he is nearby.

WHAT MAKES A CIVILIAN DOG OF COURAGE?

As you've already learned, many Dogs of Courage have special training: They learn how to sniff out clues to an arson or how to search for a missing person in the wilderness or a collapsed building. However, just because a dog hasn't been trained in a professional sense doesn't mean he can't be a Dog of Courage. On the contrary, "civilian" dogs can be even more remarkable in their heroics simply because it comes from deep within the canine psyche.

They all have in common unconditional love for and loyalty to the people in their lives, which more often than not extends to total strangers who enter the same orbit. No matter what heroic deed they perform or lives they save — whether human or animal — civilian Dogs of Courage inspire us. They also don't give up, no matter how long the odds or difficult the journey. That's because they draw on pure instinct that has developed through thousands of years of working side by side with humans.

Here are some stories that underscore how great civilian Dogs of Courage are, despite their lack of formal education.

Unconditional Love and Loyalty

Dogs have served as loving and loyal companions to countless generations of humans through the centuries. Even the Greek philosopher Homer recognized these admirable traits in his epic work *The Odyssey*. After Odysseus returned home after twenty long years away at war, no one greeted him or even recognized him. In fact, the only living creature who did recognize him was his faithful dog, Argos.

Consider Shep, a dog in Fort Benton, Montana, who first showed up at the train station in town in 1936. Workers at the depot hadn't seen him before, but the dog greeted the arrival of every train that pulled into the station. Soon, one of the employees made the connection that the first day he saw the dog was the same day that a casket containing the body of a local resident was put on the train to ship back east.

Essentially, Shep continued to visit the train station in anticipation of greeting his returning owner.

Once the depot workers realized this, they started to feed and care for Shep. He stuck around the station more than before, but he still ran to each incoming train to check for his best friend every day until he met his own end six years later.

In Japan in the 1920s there was a similar dog remarkable for his loyalty. Hachiko, an Akita, faithfully met his owner, Professor Hidesaburo Ueno, at Shibuya Station at the end of each workday when Ueno returned from his job at the University of Tokyo. When the dog was just a year and a half old, the professor was struck with a cerebral hemorrhage while at work.

Hachiko never gave up. For nine years, the dog returned to the station to patiently wait for his owner at the same time each day. Soon commuters noticed and often brought food for

ZOEY

When you see a headline that reads "Chihuahua vs. Rattlesnake" or "Toddler vs. Rattlesnake," it might seem easy to assume that the story will have an unhappy ending. Except not in this case, thanks to Zoey, a five-pound Chihuahua just under a year old, who lived in Masonville, Colorado, a small town outside of Fort Collins.

One day Denise and Monty Long were babysitting their year-old grandson at the home they shared with four dogs, of which Zoey was the smallest. Zoey and the toddler, named Booker West, were playing together in the backyard while the grandparents were inside. All of a sudden, Monty heard the dog yelp, and he and Denise rushed outside, where they were greeted by a horrendous, surreal sight.

A rattlesnake was coiled in the grass, about to strike the boy. But before the snake hit, the dog jumped in between the boy and the snake ended up biting Zoey on the head. Monty ran toward dog, boy, and snake, which looked like it was about to strike again, this time right at Booker.

Monty grabbed the boy, gathered up Zoey, and he and Denise jumped in the car and sped to a veterinarian in nearby Loveland, who administered emergency treatment to the dog.

Poor Zoey was almost unrecognizable; her head had swelled up to twice its normal size and she almost died. But the treatments worked, and Zoey was little worse for wear, save for a small scar across the top of her head. A couple of days later, she had recovered fully, much to the delight of the Longs and Booker.

"Zoey is just a very sweet dog and she loves children, but she just doesn't know she's a little dog," said Denise. "We loved her before, but [now] she's absolutely our favorite dog."*

*John C. Ensslin, "Chihuahua Champ Takes One for Toddler: Small Dog with Big Heart Saves Tot from Rattlesnake," *Rocky Mountain News*, July 23, 2007.

the Akita. At the end of each day, Hachiko returned to the house he had shared with Ueno, though it had long ago been sold to another family. One day, a former student of Ueno's traced Hachiko's path, and after talking to the new owners of the house he wrote a story about the dog's daily vigil at the train station. The story of Hachiko spread throughout the country, and he became famous.

Hachiko continued to visit the train station each day to wait for Ueno until his own death in 1934. But by then he had become so celebrated that his body was stuffed and mounted and became part of the permanent collection at the National Science Museum of Japan in Tokyo.

The loyalty of dogs is summed up in a famous speech that became an official part of the Congressional Record, though it first appeared as part of a legal argument in a case in 1870. George Graham Vest, a lawyer in Warrensburg, Missouri, was hired by a man who was suing a neighbor for damages for killing his dog. Though some thought the lawsuit was frivolous, Vest announced that he'd "win the case or apologize to every dog in Missouri." The stirring monologue won Vest the case for his client. The speech was published in various newspapers here and there, but it wasn't until Clement C. Dickinson, a congressman from Missouri, read "Eulogy on the Dog" into the Congressional Record on October 14, 1916, that it truly caught fire and would eventually become an age-old homage to loyal canines everywhere.

Here's the speech in its entirety:

Gentlemen of the jury: The best friend a man has in this world may turn against him and become his enemy. His son or daughter that he has reared with loving care may prove ungrateful. Those who are nearest and dearest to us, those whom we trust with our happiness and our good name, may become traitors to their faith. The money that a man has, he may lose. It flies away from him, perhaps when he needs it the most. A man's reputation may be sacrificed in a moment of ill-considered action. The people who are prone to fall on their knees to do us honor when success is with us may be the first to throw the stone of malice when failure settles its cloud upon our heads. The one absolutely unselfish friend that a man can have in this selfish world, the one that never deserts him and the one that never proves ungrateful or treacherous is his dog.

Gentlemen of the jury: A man's dog stands by him in prosperity and in poverty, in health and in sickness. He will sleep on the cold ground, where the wintry winds blow and the snow drives fiercely, if only he may be near his master's side. He will kiss the hand that has no food to offer, he will lick the wounds and sores that come in encounters with the roughness of the world. He guards the sleep of his pauper master as if he were a prince. When all other friends desert, he remains. When riches *take wings and reputation falls to pieces, he is as constant in his love as the sun in its journey through the heavens.*

If fortune drives the master forth an outcast in the world, friendless and homeless, the faithful dog asks no higher privilege than that of accompanying him to guard against danger, to fight against his enemies, and when the last scene of all comes, and death takes the master in its embrace and his body is laid away in the cold ground, no matter if all other friends pursue their way, there by his graveside will the noble dog be found, his head between his paws, his eyes sad but open in alert watchfulness, faithful and true even to death.

Injury Doesn't Stop Them

Dogs have shown a remarkable ability to forge ahead despite debilitating injuries or disabilities. We've all seen three-legged canines and dogs who are deaf or blind carry on in their daily lives as though it's the norm, while many humans would be felled with much less of a disability.

That's because for them, their disability becomes the norm. After a brief period of adjustment, they continue on as before because they have no choice and don't think that they're supposed to act differently.

256

Take a mastiff mixed breed in Jacksonville, Florida, who had been shot in the chest and was found behind a convenience store. Despite his injury, he was trying to walk by dragging himself along by his front legs. A customer brought him to a local humane organization where workers determined that a bullet had grazed the dog's spinal cord, causing his paralysis.

Tammy Scott, the vet tech on duty at the time, thought he might have to be put down. "He just sat there with this stoic look on his face and all he could do was just move his front legs," she said.

Against the veterinarian's orders, Scott decided to treat the dog with steroids and see how he was feeling the next day. "The next morning, it was like he said, 'Okay, you're back. I'm ready,'" Scott said. "By the end of the 24 hours, he was like a different dog."[3]

He needed a name and Bullet was the obvious choice. Then they found him a special wheelchair, made from a modified two-wheel cart found at a local thrift store. But as it turned out, he wouldn't need it for long. Within a couple of months Bullet could walk without the cart, and six months after he was injured, the dog could run down the street. In the wake of his amazing recovery, Scott decided to adopt Bullet.

257

"Usually when a dog gets into that situation a lot of them give up, so it's just the strength and the willingness to want to recover, to want to live a normal life," said Scott. "You don't see that determination very often."[4]

Harper, a pit bull, not only triumphed over extreme adversity but also inspired thousands of people to persevere in their own lives regardless of the obstacles that were thrown before them.

One day in the summer of 2011, a woman in Sanford, Florida, happened upon a man in the parking lot of a grocery store who was selling pit bull puppies for $50 each. She noticed a trash bag off to the side, with a puppy thrashing around in it. When she asked about the puppy, the man at first didn't want to talk about it, but when the woman insisted, he handed her the bag.

Inside, she saw a puppy lying on her stomach, limbs splayed out to the sides. The dog was unable to hold up her head. The woman brought the bag to the local animal shelter, and employees and a veterinarian agreed that it was best to euthanize the dog.

Erica Daniel, a woman active in the local animal rescue community, had recently created Dolly's Foundation to rescue and find new homes for pit bulls and similar breeds, and she happened to be at the shelter that day. When she asked about the puppy, a vet explained that she had "swimmer puppy syndrome," or *pectus excavatum,* a condition that usually proves fatal in puppies. Euthanization was scheduled for the following day.

Daniel agreed with the staff but asked to take the puppy home for one night. "I had to show her what it was like to be loved," she said. "I'd planned on taking her home that night, letting her sleep in bed with us, and having her humanely euthanized in the morning."

Once she took the puppy home, Daniel made her as comfortable as possible, massaging her torso and legs and petting her. That's when the puppy surprised everyone.

She tried to lift her head and actually succeeded in getting it off the ground enough so she could look around. Then, the puppy tried to stand up. Though she couldn't heave herself up entirely, she was able to boost herself a little bit.

Daniel was amazed. She canceled the euthanization, although the vet warned her against it, citing other health problems that can plague a dog as a result of swimmer puppy syndrome. Daniel convinced the vet to test for these conditions, and to everyone's surprise — and relief — the puppy came away with a clean bill of health. All she had to do was to build up her muscle strength. With a combination of continuing massage sessions and hydrotherapy at a local canine center that specializes in treating dogs through swim therapy sessions, soon Harper was able to walk and even run.[5]

"She's a big goofball!" said Daniel. "She's a typical puppy. She's eaten a couple of pairs of shoes. But she's awesome. We love her so much. I just look forward to waking up and seeing her face every day."[6]

THEY INSPIRE US

Many dogs never get a second chance. Those dogs who are granted another chance are sometimes so grateful that they go on to achieve great things by helping other people — sometimes just by making them smile — and in turn inspiring others to do likewise.

Marvin, a goofy black Lab, was just one of those dogs. Even though E. J. Finocchio, a veterinarian and president of the Rhode Island SPCA, was quite familiar with less-than-perfect dogs and how their outlooks and temperaments weren't affected by a mere disability, such a dog wasn't on his radar when he wandered through the shelter's dog kennels to look for a dog to serve as a companion at home for his wife when he had to travel.

SHEBA

An eighteen-month-old rottweiler named Sheba turned into a fierce warrior when she rescued nine of her newborn puppies after her owner had buried them in a two-foot-deep grave because they weren't purebred.

Sheba belonged to Robert Homrighous of Oakland Park, Florida, a suburb of Fort Lauderdale. He had hoped to sell the pure-bred puppies. So after Sheba gave birth to nine puppies, and Homrighous took one look at them — a mix of rottweiler, chow, and Labrador retriever — he got out a shovel, started digging in his backyard, and buried them alive only yards away from Sheba's doghouse. Sheba — chained up to a nearby tree — saw everything and started barking and scratching at the ground, and wouldn't stop for the next twelve hours.

Several neighbors called the police. When they arrived, including Sergeant Sherry Schlueter of the Broward County Sheriff Department, they found that Sheba had broken free of her chain and was digging up puppies.

"He doesn't believe in spaying or neutering, but he does believe in burying his dogs alive and killing them," said Schlueter, who rushed them to a nearby animal hospital.*

"They were a little dehydrated, and they all had a lot of sand in them," said Dr. Cindi Bossart, the veterinarian who treated Sheba and her puppies; unfortunately three of the puppies didn't survive the ordeal. "The fact that they're even here today is a real miracle."†

The mother "obviously knew what was going on and what happened," said Schlueter. "This dog is really quite a hero as far as I'm concerned."‡

Afterward, Homrighous was vilified across the country, and rightfully so. "There have been hundreds, even thousands of letters to Bob and to me, those that say I'm going to kill you for it, those who say I'm going to kill your lawyer for it," said Guy Seligman, his attorney.

Homrighous pleaded no contest to three counts of animal cruelty and six counts of animal abandonment and was sentenced to four months in jail and five years probation for cruelty to animals.§

"Sheba is a remarkable dog," said Sergeant Schlueter. "In my opinion, the dog suffered terribly trying to get free to save her infants."[¶]

---
*"Mama Dog Rescues Her Buried Pups," *Albany Times Union,* January 18, 1995.
[†]Ibid.
[‡]Ibid.
[§]"Man Who Buried Puppies Draws Jail Term," *Albany Times Union,* April 29, 1995.
[¶]Ibid.

But when he locked eyes with Marvin, he realized that this dog was destined for his family despite his history.

"Marvin was twice homeless, lonely and unwanted, once because his first owners no longer had time for him, and his second family no longer wanted him because of his limp," said Dr. Finocchio. "He lived in cage 15 at the RISPCA, a cinder-block area, for months waiting for his second chance for doing nothing. We decided to give it a shot and on Thanksgiving Day, 2002, Marvin came home for dinner as our 15th invited guest and never left."[7]

It didn't take long for Marvin to insinuate himself not only into the Finocchio family's life but also into the community as a whole. He accompanied Finocchio to work and soon became the de facto canine ambassador for the SPCA.

The veterinarian and dog trained together to become a therapy dog team, and soon they began to visit hospitals. The human part of the team said his eyes were opened as never before. "Marvin brought me to the other side of the tracks and introduced me to a world of loneliness, sickness, disability and deprivation," said Finocchio. "He taught me that doing little things such as visiting an elderly person in a nursing home meant so much to that person or having a sick child pat him on the head made that child forget about their illness. To the world he was just someone but to many lonely people he was the world when he visited them. He taught me that people complicate their lives and fail to cherish how fortunate they are at day's end. I never once forgot about how fortunate I was once Marvin entered my life."[8]

Marvin's generous spirit didn't end there. Finocchio set up a charitable nonprofit organization called the Marvin Fund, which helped people who were disabled or elderly who were struggling financially and in danger of losing their pets. The fund gave them pet food and financial assistance to help pay vet bills. To help raise money for the Marvin Fund, the dog turned to creating paintings to be sold. MarvArt, as it was known, was a no-brainer: Nontoxic watercolor paint was applied to Marvin's tail and a canvas placed underneath it. Once he started wagging his tail, he created masterpieces that tended toward the impressionistic. Marvin's paintings were presented at local art festivals, given away to other nonprofits so they could sell them and raise money, and even displayed at the Rhode Island Water Color Society, a highly notable honor for any painter, with two legs or otherwise.

As if this weren't enough, Marvin also wrote *Marvelous Marvin,* a book about his many adventures, to raise money for the fund. According to Finocchio, the Marvin Fund has helped more than fifteen hundred people keep their pets. Marvin passed away in early 2010, but the fund will continue to help people in the state and inspire people all over the world.

Faith is another dog who has served as a real inspiration to countless humans. One day in late 2002, Jude Stringfellow's son brought her a small puppy who wasn't expected to survive. The reason: The dog was born with only three legs and her mother had tried to smother her by lying on her.

At first, Stringfellow, a single mom of three kids in Oklahoma City, said absolutely not.

She was already having a tough time economically, and taking care of the dog they already had was a problem.

But her son persisted, and Stringfellow thought the dog at least deserved a fighting chance, though both she and the veterinarian she consulted didn't think the dog would survive due to the weakness in her back legs and her respiratory problems because of her mother's actions.

They named the dog Faith, and the scrappy pup did much more than live up to her name.

"We put peanut butter on the end of a spoon and held it above nose level," said Stringfellow. "She'd try to lick it and fall over, like any other toddler. Eventually her back legs became strong enough to sit up like a squirrel, then her belly muscles became stronger so she could sit straight up."

A few weeks later, Faith went into the backyard, which was heaped with snow. But that didn't stop her; she took a few tentative hops, and then made her way around the yard like she had been doing it forever. When she got back inside, she hopped from room to room, over furniture, across obstacles. At that point, Stringfellow knew she had a special dog.

"I'd watch her play with the other dogs

REAGAN

Throughout history, while it's been true that many dogs are not overly fond of cats, some learn to tolerate them and keep the peace for the sake of their human companions.

One yellow Lab in Des Moines, Iowa, who goes by the name of Reagan not only tolerates cats but even helped to save the lives of two three-week-old kittens who had been abandoned by the side of a heavily trafficked road and intentionally left to die.

Kerry, Reagan's owner, had learned to put up with the dog's tendency to drag stray items and occasionally a piece of trash from the neighborhood into the backyard and keep watch over the objects until the next thing caught his eye. So she didn't think the presence of a crumpled-up bag of Meow Mix was out of place one day when she returned from work.

But Reagan's behavior that particular day was out of character. While he typically greeted and accompanied Kerry into the house after her long day at work, he acted differently, whining and hovering near the empty bag of cat food, and refusing to go inside.

She opened the bag. To her horror, what she found was not a few crumbs of dry cat food but instead two squirming, crying kittens covered with blood and the crushed bodies of their littermates. Kerry brought the bag inside and cleaned them up as best she could, but she soon realized they needed special care. So the next day she called several shelters and humane associations, and Linda Blakely of the Raccoon Valley Animal Sanctuary and Rescue in Des Moines took them in.

The two surviving kittens were named Tipper and Skipper, and as is usually the case with a high-profile rescued-animal story, offers to adopt the kittens poured in.

"Skipper and Tipper have definitely touched the world's hearts and they do need homes, but there are Skipper and Tipper situations in every shelter across the country," Blakely said. "Keep that soft spot in your heart and go to your local shelter."*

At the same time, she honored Reagan's spirit and lifesaving actions. "The instinct of the dog was to nurture and not kill the kittens," said Blakely. "With all the blood, and she didn't care that she didn't have [four] legs. They didn't care either."[9]

Soon word began to spread about the courageous little dog. Her one front leg started to wither away and weaken, and Stringfellow decided to have the leg amputated when Faith was around seven months old. After a quick recuperation, the dog was back to hopping around — and would eventually learn to walk — as well as inspiring people.

They began to visit people who needed inspiration, in hospitals, schools, and nursing homes. One day they visited Walter Reed Army Medical Center and spent time with Frankie, a soldier who had served in Iraq and lost both legs as the result of an IED. Frankie was deeply depressed; he loved being a soldier — it had been his lifelong dream — and now not only could he not serve in the military, he couldn't walk. No one could reach him, he was that withdrawn.

269

When he first met Faith, he sat up in bed. She walked right into the room as if nothing was wrong. The soldier saw a dog who acted like she could conquer the world despite having only two legs.

"I know he was absolutely moved," said Stringfellow. "He said, 'I know if a dog can do it, I can do it.'" He kept in touch with Jude to ask after Faith and to keep them posted on his own progress. Soon he was fitted with a pair of prosthetic legs, and when he was discharged from the hospital, he called them.

Jude remembers the conversation well. "He said, 'I'm walking out of the hospital, put Faith on the phone.'"[10]

Another time, Faith and Jude were in New York City walking down the street when they saw a woman in a wheelchair who called them over.

"She was crying and said she had seen Faith on television," said Jude. The woman was diabetic and had lost her legs. "She just held Faith and said she wished she had that kind of courage. Then she told us that she was on [her] way to pick up a gun. She handed the pawn ticket to a police officer and said she didn't need it anymore."[11]

This type of emotional reaction has become the rule whenever Faith walks into a room. Faith and Jude often visit military bases, and Stringfellow says it is these visits that are especially poignant.

"She just walks around barking and laughing and excited to see them all," said Jude. "There is a lot of crying, pointing and surprise. From those who have lost friends or limbs, there can be silence. Some will shake my hand and thank me, others will pat her on the head. There is a lot of quiet, heartfelt, really deep emotion."[12]

They Keep Us from Harm

Dogs operate with such keen instincts and extreme sense of loyalty, it leads them to act first and think later if one of their human companions is in trouble.

In Kansas City, a woman had learned to live with an abusive partner, hiding it from others as best she could, accepting that this was how life was for her and maybe eventually the abuse would stop. However, one day the man's physical attacks caused her to reach the breaking point and she started to scream.

"When my Great Dane heard me scream, he laid on top of me," said the woman. "I tried to get him out of the way, but he received the first of many blows."

In an instant, the dog turned the tables and attacked the man, who became enraged and began to attack the dog before hurling him off the front porch. The woman rushed to the dog, but her abuser warned her he'd shoot the dog if she got any closer. She didn't know whether to believe him, so instead she ran to a neighbor's house to call for help.

Police soon arrived and arrested the man. After they took him away, the woman returned to the house to find her beloved dog motionless. With the help of the police, they brought the dog to a local veterinarian, who diagnosed the Great Dane with several broken ribs and a broken hip.

She called a local shelter for abused women, and they invited her to stay with them but told her she couldn't bring her dog. She turned them down because he had saved her life and told them that they'd sleep in her car instead.

The center considered this and decided to allow the woman to stay at the shelter with her dog. "Because of her incredibly dangerous situation, we made an exception for her and her dog," said Susan Miller, CEO of the Rose Brooks Center that welcomed her.[13]

"It's difficult to imagine the amount of courage it must have taken for a dog to deliberately put himself in such a horrifying scenario," said Anne Sterling, Midwest regional director of the Humane Society of the United States. "The dog did it without hesitation, demonstrating once again the undeniable intelligence and compassionate nature present in animals."[14]

In fact, from that point on, the center began to develop plans to expand the shelter by building a separate wing to accommodate owners and their pets.

Then there's Titan, a pit bull in Atlanta who saved the life of a woman who would have likely died of a brain aneurysm if he didn't take action.

It all started one morning in July 2011 when John Benton was about to leave the house to go to work. He typically saw Titan off with a quick pat to the head before he headed out the door, but this day the dog wouldn't settle for the usual good-bye.

"He ran down the steps and would not let me go out the front door," said Benton. "He was barking and running around in circles, and he'd run up a few flights of steps and run back down just to keep me from going, to let me know something was wrong. And that's when I followed him up the stairs to see what he was trying to tell me."

There he found his wife, Gloria, lying on the floor, bleeding from the head. He called 911 and they rushed her to the hospital.

Later, doctors told Benton that his wife had a brain aneurysm, which had caused her to fall, fracturing her skull.

Gloria survived and Titan was named Neighbor of the Year by the Vintage Pointe Neighborhood Association where they live.[15]

THEY DON'T GIVE UP

Dogs of Courage persevere when others would easily give up. Take Lucky, a mix of Alsatian shepherd and Labrador who was lost in the Italian Alps in the middle of winter for an astounding ten days and survived.

Winter hiking is popular in the thickly wooded region, and after several hikers called the local forestry department to report that they heard the whimpering of a dog, a search team was sent out. After several attempts, the workers called off their search, only to be summoned back by more hikers who also had heard the sounds of a dog lost nearby. The search went on and off for a full ten days before the dog was located.

"I could hear a dog whining and whimpering for help but it took me ages to actually find him as he was half covered with snow," said Massimo Gianoli, the rescuer who ultimately found the dog. "The conditions were appalling and it was very cold, but I followed the sound of the whimpering and then I saw his dark coat poking out from the snow; he had actually been very clever and found a little bit of shelter by some rocks. I gave him an energy bar and he quickly ate it and then I activated my GPS which allowed the other teams to find me."[16]

Lucky was treated by a local veterinarian and made a full recovery.

On the other side of the world, near Libertyville, Illinois, the efforts of another equally persistent dog helped save the life of a woman who had fallen into a river and was in danger of dying of hypothermia or drowning.

Margo Milde, an avid bird-watcher, was surveying birds on New Year's Day in 1998 to help out with the yearly National Audubon Society census. She was walking along the Des Plaines River when she slipped on the edge and into the river, which had a depth of four to seven feet and temperatures near freezing.

Fortunately, she happened to fall in near Gene Eich's backyard, where his dog, Willie, heard her and started to bark. In fact, he wouldn't let up, which caused Eich to check out the cause of his barking. He headed for the river, slogging through the woods for some 120 yards, where he spotted Milde.

"I heard a woman's voice and I looked over,

and there was a woman in the water," he said. "She was up to her chest in the water and was holding on to a root in the bank. She kept sinking." Eich and other neighbors who had heard the commotion sprang into action. "I didn't know how long we could hold her, but we never let her go."

Eich's wife, Tammy, had followed her husband to the river and rushed back to the house to call 911. Firefighters rescued Milde, but Eich gives credit to his dog for serving as the spark.

"Willie really set off the alarm, so to speak," Eich said. "I'd have never gone back into the woods if he didn't keep barking."[17]

CHAPTER ELEVEN: CELEBRITY DOGS OF COURAGE

Some Dogs of Courage become famous because of their heroic actions. But a select few become Dogs of Courage simply *because* they're famous. After all, whether or not you have a dog in your own life, who doesn't like to see a compelling story on the silver screen of a dog whose sole priority is to save the people in his life?

Or, in a variation on the theme, a canine actor who serves as a comic foil, either on a TV show or in a movie, who makes people laugh and helps them to forget their troubles, at least for a little while?

A celebrity Dog of Courage may not have prevented a person from meeting certain death in real life, but he is still a vital part of the culture. Besides, his courageous on-screen actions — or antics — may just help to inspire people out in the real world to be kinder to both two- and four-legged creatures.

Celebrity Dogs of Courage have been around since the silent movies of the early twentieth century, when a dog often served as sidekick to stars such as Charlie Chaplin or Buster Keaton — even for just one scene. In fact, both actors were canny enough to know that having a dog in the picture would inevitably help to draw in the crowds. In the very first scene of Chaplin's 1915 movie *The Champion,* the star is shown as his Little Tramp character sharing a hot dog with a bulldog, who appears as his sidekick throughout the film and even plays a pivotal role in the main fight scene. The film was a hit and Chaplin learned his lesson. In fact, some film historians argue that he really made his name in *A Dog's Life,* a 1918 movie where he builds on his Little Tramp character and joins forces with a mutt named Scraps. In the story, both man and dog are homeless and have to scrape for a living, but in the end they triumph over adversity.

Dogs have been stealing movie scenes from humans young and old ever since. In 1917, Teddy the Wonder Dog rescued damsel-in-distress Gloria Swanson from the railroad tracks in *Teddy at the Throttle,* though he made his debut as a contract player with

278

Mack Sennett's Keystone Film Company in the 1913 movie *A Little Hero*. In 1923, *Where the North Begins* not only made Rin Tin Tin a star, but it turned out to be one of the hottest movies of the year. In fact, it was so popular that in addition to being the spark that launched Rin Tin Tin's career, it spawned what has become an endless stream of dog-hero movies, starring canines such as Lassie, Old Yeller, Benji, and even Air Bud.

However, Celebrity Dogs of Courage got their start even earlier in England, where a dog named Rover starred in the 1905 six-minute movie *Rescued by Rover*.

Diana Schaub put it best: "Faithful as always, dogs keep trying to restore our heroism to us. In almost every dog movie I can think of, the dog serves as the source of instruction for various benighted, misguided, or simply young humans, especially boys. Boys need an education in the manly virtues that only a boy's dog can give. By movie's end, the dog has readied the boy for his passage into manhood. In the best dog movies, that rite of passage usually includes the loss of the dog and a confrontation with mortality."[1]

TRAINING

Celebrity Dogs of Courage can make us laugh or cry, but it takes an incredible amount of work and training to get to the point where their acting looks natural.

Finding a special kind of dog who can become successful in movies or TV is the easy part. The rest involves a dedicated professional animal trainer who has not only an abundance of patience but also the foresight to see the innate talent and personality in a dog when first setting eyes on him.

"There's no difference between a common house pet and an animal superstar except the trainers," said Karl Lewis Miller, who trained dogs for the films *Cujo* and *Beethoven*. "It's having an animal in the right place at the right time with the person who has the experience and the expertise to teach an animal to do it. An animal is as good or as bad as his trainer. Sure, there is something special about the animal, but only because it's brought out by the person teaching him."[2]

"Your neighbor's dalmatian could have been Lassie, if that's what the script had called for," Miller continued. "But he would have needed Rudd Weatherwax to develop him into that great dog."[3]

At the same time, the dog has to look like he's interacting with the human actor in front of him in a movie or on a Broadway stage, and not with a trainer offstage, so a dog's costars also have to learn how to work with a dog. Larry Madrid, animal trainer for movies including *Marley & Me,* believes this is the most difficult aspect of training any animal actor. "When you're watching the movie, you don't want to think about 'Oh, he's looking [off camera] at the trainer,'" he said. "If you can watch the movie and not think about the fact that it's a trained animal who is looking at the trainer, I've done my job."[4]

In addition to talent and natural charisma, a dog — like his human actor counterparts — needs to be able to tune out the many distractions that are typical on a movie soundstage or TV set. There are bright lights, lots of people milling around, and occasionally loud noises and people yelling at each other, whether among the production staff or the actors, for real or as part of the script.

Once a dog passes the initial tests — correct breed, size, and color, and personality to spare — the serious training begins. When the camera's rolling, the last thing a director wants to hear is a dog trainer calling out commands — the same goes for the audience at a Broadway show with a canine actor — so trainers have to rely on hand signals and facial expressions to tell the canine star what to do, often from across the room.

Depending upon the production, training

may take a couple of weeks for simple shows or up to a year for more complex movies that rely on a dog as a main character and may require numerous stand-ins at a variety of ages over the course of a movie — like *Marley & Me,* for example, which was based on the best-selling book about the irrepressible chew-everything-in-sight yellow Labrador retriever. Because the movie dealt with Marley at all stages of his life, acquiring and training suitable canines for the movie was a gargantuan task. Not only did they need dogs — and several stand-ins — for each stage of his life, from puppyhood to old age, but the dogs needed to be able to channel their inner Marleys, and on cue.

Mark Forbes, head trainer on the film, had previously worked on *101 Dalmatians,* among other movies, but Marley presented unique challenges. "It was different from any movie we'd really done before in that this was supposed to be the most out-of-control, rambunctious dog there ever was," said Forbes. "And so we definitely looked for, in each team, a dog that had that personality trait. [On] our 1- to 5-year-old team, we had five dogs. And we had Ziggy. 'Crystal Meth,' they called him when we brought him on the set. He was just a crazy dog. And then we had Clyde, who was sort of 'Trained Crystal

Meth,' but just had a wild streak in him."

Though Forbes and other trainers had worked diligently to train the dogs, they quickly realized that they had to throw out the playbook in order to make the movie while remaining true to Marley's spirit and instincts.

"I remember the very first day we had a scene where Jen [Aniston] is bringing Marley home, and we were using Clyde and we rehearsed it. She unclipped him, and he ran in, he jumped up on the kitchen table, did a circle, licked Owen in the face and ran out of the room. From that day forward, the director David Frankel would never let us rehearse, especially Clyde. We'd just let [the dogs] go do what they were going to do in their own little Marley way."[5]

In all, twenty-two Labs were required over the course of filming the movie, and Larry Madrid, another trainer who worked on the film, discloses a secret about making an animal movie: Not only are a variety of dogs needed to satisfy the birth-to-death life cycle of the canine star, they also need to have different temperaments: crazy, shy, even-tempered.

For instance, yellow Lab Jonah was used in scenes where Marley had to be relatively calm. Madrid referred to him as "Mellow

EDDIE

Eddie, the Jack Russell terrier who often upstaged his human counterparts on the much-beloved and long-running TV series *Frasier,* had an auspicious entry into the world.

Named Moose by Sam and Connie Thise because he was the biggest of his siblings born on Christmas Eve 1989, his owners sold the rest of the litter but kept him. "He's wild," said Connie. "He could climb trees, straight up for about 6 feet. And he loved to roll around in cow manure — especially after we bathed him."*

After a while, Moose proved to be too rambunctious for the Thises, but Connie thought his energy and curiosity would serve him well in show biz. Cathy Morrison, an animal trainer who worked at Universal Studios Florida, agreed and took him on.

"He was hard to train because he was incorrigible," said Morrison. "You'd come home and you'd find him up on the table. He would have eaten something on the table. Or he was ripping into something. All the time, some kind of mischief."†

Morrison had been working with Moose for eighteen months when word spread that the producers of *Frasier* were looking for a dog for the show. She and Moose showed up at the audition, and they won the part.

Trainer Mathilde De Cagny took over, and it didn't take long for Moose — now named Eddie for the show — to make his mark. "Some days he's more hyper, some days less," said De Cagny. "But he's a very smart dog. It doesn't take him more than two weeks to learn a trick, usually less."[‡]

Soon Moose was pulling in $10,000 for each episode of *Frasier,* and he got more fan mail than any of the other cast members. But they didn't mind that he stole most of the scenes he appeared in, because his popularity just meant that more people would watch the show.

Most of the credit for Moose's on-screen persona was due to De Cagny. "We're like an old married couple," she said. "I'm 10 feet away from him at all times, and there's a lot of silent communication between us, with hand signals and eye contact that only the live audience can see."

Moose stayed on the show for ten years, to much acclaim. He even penned — pawed? — his own autobiography, *My Life as a Dog.*

"Moose is a wonderful actor and is a lot better behaved than most actors in Hollywood," said De Cagny.[§]

Moose/Eddie died on June 28, 2006, at the ripe old age of sixteen. Toward the end of the show's run, his son Enzo — almost the spitting image of his father — started to fill in for his dad on the show, helped along by a little makeup to match the brown spot on his back.

---

[*]Linda Shrieves, "Eddie, the Dog on 'Frasier,' Is a Star and a Handful," *Orlando Sentinel,* December 16, 1993.
[†]Ibid.
[‡]"The Star with the Irresistible Look Can Be a Pistol of a Pooch," *Seattle Post-Intelligencer,* April 1, 1999.
[§]"Frasier Dog Has Natural Talent," Associated Press, September 12, 1999.

Marley." "He's a nice quiet Marley who'll sit in the background and not cause trouble for the actors when they're doing a scene that isn't really about him," Madrid explained.[6]

Using multiple dogs throughout filming presented unexpected challenges: At least two of the puppies were female. As a result, some digital cinema enhancement was necessary.

"[In one scene], Owen is holding the puppy by its front legs and its belly's hanging down," said Forbes. "David Frankel showed it to his wife, [who said], 'That's not a boy puppy.' So they actually put a digital wee-wee on the little puppy."[7]

Not only are there the time-consuming aspects of getting the dog to do the trick — or *not* — but when more than one critter shares the billing, the fur can certainly fly. At the very least, the training regimen takes longer in order to allow time for the animal costars to become acquainted with — and tolerate — each other, even if it's only for the sake of appearances.

The trainer Mathilde De Cagny worked on the 1996 film *Homeward Bound II: Lost in San Francisco,* starring Shadow, a golden retriever; Chance, an American bulldog; and Sassy, a Himalayan cat. She was in charge of training Clovis and Martel, the two dogs who would play Shadow. She said that unlike the story line in the movie, it was far from love at first sight when all of the canine actors playing Chance and Shadow met for the first time.

"We had to do a lot of training to put the dogs together," she said. "Once they were trained, it was fine. But at first, everybody was kept on a leash because they wouldn't accept each other."

De Cagny prefers working with older dogs. "Getting them when they're older gives you the advantage of knowing what they're about," she said. "Puppies, although cute, are thoroughly unpredictable."[8]

RIN TIN TIN

Dogs of Courage from almost a century ago paved the way for today's canine stars. And unlike Marley and other contemporary canine actors, the road to stardom for these earlier dogs was typically fraught with peril.

Indeed, this was the case for Rin Tin Tin, widely considered the world's first real canine movie star, though he wound up in a very different place from where he started out. In fact, it was a miracle he survived puppyhood to become an icon.

The puppy was born just two months before World War I ended; his mother had given birth in a kennel that had been virtually destroyed by bombs in Lorraine, France. Lee Duncan, an American soldier, scooped up him and his sister, the only other surviving littermate, when they were just days old, and he named them Rintintin and Nénette after two popular French dolls. Duncan nursed them to health at the army camp and brought them back to the States with him when the war ended.

Unfortunately, Nénette didn't survive, but Duncan put everything into training her

288

brother, whom he had started to call Rinty. The dog learned tricks quickly, and Duncan started showing him off at dog shows, where Rinty had no trouble jumping eleven feet through the air. One of Duncan's friends filmed Rinty's stunts with an experimental motion picture camera, and once Duncan saw the results he began to make plans to help Rin Tin Tin become a star.

It didn't take long. Duncan spent countless hours training the dog and making the rounds of Hollywood movie studios after the war. Rinty's first role was playing the bit part of a wolf in a 1922 movie *The Man from Hell's River.* His big break came the following year when he starred in *Where the North Begins,* which sold out in theaters all across the country, and from that point on Rinty was a bona fide movie star, traveling across the country, "signing" thousands of autographed photos with his paw print, and hobnobbing with human celebrities, including Jean Harlow.

America couldn't get enough of this Dog of Courage. Rin Tin Tin made a total of twenty-six movies for Warner Bros. — his popularity supposedly helped the studio avoid bankruptcy — and his weekly salary was $1,000. Plus, he started to do a weekly radio series. Duncan knew that his best friend couldn't last forever, however, so he bred Rinty to ensure a successor, something that would be sorely needed as the Great Depression hit.

Rinty died in 1932, and his son Rin Tin Tin Jr. stepped in, ensuring that stories of this heroic dog would continue to be told. In 1947, *The Return of Rin Tin Tin* debuted on the big screen, starring a young Robert Blake in his first big-screen role. The common thread throughout most of the Rin Tin Tin stories is this: Lonely, possibly orphaned boy meets dog. Dog heals boy, who is now happy. Dog and boy ride off into the sunset. This was the case in *The Return of Rin Tin Tin* and countless other movies starring the German shepherd. Perhaps this recurring theme is no surprise given Duncan's own childhood, during which he spent three years in an or-phanage where he never stopped looking for a hero.

Rin Tin Tin made his TV debut in 1954, and the series ran for five years. He earned his star on the Hollywood Walk of Fame in 1960. The line continued not only beyond the dog's death and the subsequent deaths of his many offspring, but also beyond Duncan's death in 1960. A variety of breeders and managers took over the care, feeding, and training of future Rin Tin Tins, and in 2012, the twelfth in line was still actively promoting the ideals of this iconic Dog of Courage by serving as an ambassador with the American Humane Association, making public appearances, and generally providing hope to people all over the world.

Best-selling author Susan Orlean devoted an entire book to his story. *Rin Tin Tin: The Life and the Legend* describes the dog as "an idea and an ideal — a hero who was also a friend, a fighter who was also a caretaker, a mute genius, a companionable loner. He was one dog and many dogs, a real animal and an invented character, a pet as well as an international celebrity. He was born in 1918 and he never died."[9]

LASSIE

Like Rin Tin Tin, the planets had to align for the dog who would come to play Lassie. When MGM was casting for its 1943 movie starring a female collie, the studio was looking to build on the public's adoration of Rin Tin Tin, and then some. First, this dog would not only be a friend to orphaned boys but would also get entire families out of a jam, whether the trouble was a burned-down homestead or the economic hardships caused by a failed crop.

From the beginning, Metro-Goldwyn-Mayer planned *Lassie Come Home* to be a bigger-budget production than the Rinty franchise, with better scripts, A-list actors, and lush cinematography; Elizabeth Taylor and Roddy McDowell were already signed on to the project. And, most important, producers wanted to offer a story that didn't take place in a war zone, given the public's war fatigue at the time, two years into America's involvement in World War II.

The studio auditioned more than a thousand dogs, and Rudd Weatherwax's dog Pal had several strikes against him: First, he was male. Plus, he didn't have papers certifying he was purebred. Last, the white stripe blazed on his nose was not the standard of collie breeders of the time.

But the producers gave him a second-string part, figuring he was well trained enough to play the body double for the female lead. On one of the first days of filming, the lead Lassie was supposed to jump into a river and swim across it. But it turned out that the star was afraid of water. So they shot another take with Pal stepping in as understudy. He swam across in a determined fashion, and when he reached the bank, he crawled up the side and then really showed his acting chops. Weatherwax directed him according to the script, as being so exhausted he lacked even the energy to shake off the water. The director decided to give Pal the starring role on the spot.

Lassie Come Home was the first success in a franchise that continues to this day. Between 1943 and 1949, MGM produced five different Lassie movies; the TV series launched in 1954 and ran until 1971. And then came the remakes and updated versions of the first string of movies.

Weatherwax, Lassie's first trainer, died in 1985, but training Lassie — and other animals for film and TV — has turned into the family business. Bob Weatherwax, Rudd's son, has continued his father's legacy and painstaking pursuit of perfection, not only when it comes to training the dogs but also for Lassie's trademark look.

For one, Lassie has *never* been played by a female. Though Pal won his first role with his superior acting talents, Weatherwax soon discovered a compelling reason to stick with male dogs.

"They keep their coat better all year," explained Bob. "They shed in the summer and the females will almost shed their entire coat, where the male retains two thirds of his. And that's a lot better on film."

Unlike modern-day movies like *Marley & Me* that have anywhere from two to five dogs on hand to play one part, Lassie's trainers prided themselves on using just one. "[One dog] does everything," said Bob. "Actually, we're lucky to have gotten eight in 50 or 51 years. He has very peculiar markings and it's a genetic imperfection with the breed."[10]

There's another reason why male dogs work better on the set: "They don't have the problem of coming into season when we were on location, which would have attracted a lot of other dogs," said June Lockhart, who starred in the *Lassie* TV series from 1958 to 1964. "[Otherwise], we would have had to turn the hose on them."[11]

Because Lassie was still a female on-screen, the real dog didn't hide his disdain at having to pick up some of his character's sex-appropriate traits. "Of the 150–250 commands that Lassie knew, the one he hated was 'nurse,'" said Ace Collins, author of *Lassie: A Dog's Life*. "They would put honey on the dog's coat. The last thing Lassie wanted was puppies chewing on his coat."[12]

Lassie remakes appear about once every decade or so. Why is Lassie still so popular today? "The root of it is that dogs mean a great deal to people; they have for centuries," said Collins. "Even in today's urban world, a bond between a family and a pet is a very deep bond. Lassie represented the potential of every dog. And I think Lassie represented the best in every human being."[13]

Inevitably, when dog lovers of a certain age name the first dog movie that both made them cry and had the biggest impact on their dog-loving lives, the film cited is *Old Yeller,* based on the 1956 novel by Fred Gipson. And indeed, it's a tearjerker.

Set in the 1860s, the movie is about a boy named Travis Coates who grows up quickly when his father leaves him in charge of the farm and tells him to take care of his mother and younger brother while he heads off to work on a cattle drive for several months.

A dog soon shows up to befriend Travis, and though his mother warns against it, the boy takes a liking to the dog, who ends up helping out and even defends the family from various intruders over the course of the movie. After the dog contracts rabies while protecting the Coates family from a wolf, Travis has no choice but to shoot Old Yeller. The only thing that helps Travis is raising Old Yeller's puppy.

It's a hard film for an adult to watch, let alone young kids. One reviewer who covered the airing of the classic movie on TV steeled himself to watch it again for the first time since childhood. "In 1957, an 8-year-old-boy sat in a movie theater, watched *Old Yeller,* and was reduced to a blathering pile of Jell-

O," wrote Daniel Ruth. "Twenty-nine years later, the classic Disney film still has the same effect. If you don't believe me, try sitting through [it yourself]. Between the sobbing of parents and the weeping of the kiddos, the area around TV sets on Sunday evening will resemble the Wailing Wall."[14]

And just because you played a starring role in the film doesn't mean you're immune from the emotional wallop. "Well, yeah, there were goose bumps," said Fess Parker, who played the father. "I don't think when you get to that moment of growing up . . . well, it's difficult. I look at my own experience in life, and I tell my own children and grandchildren that it's a very tough world out there."[15]

In the end, whether it's a Celebrity Dog of Courage or an unknown mixed-breed who's the love of your life, there's only one thing that matters when it comes to dogs and what they can teach us.

"Everybody has to deal with their own mortality. Dogs make us do that," said Larry Madrid. "They bring so much pleasure to your life, but you look back at the great dogs you've had, the great times, and realize, 'Geez, they only live about 10 years.' So make the most of those years. Dogs do."[16]

NOTES

Chapter One: Dogs of Courage

1. U.S. Postal Service, January 23, 2012, press release.

2. William C. Bayne, "Officers Recount Fagan's Bravery — Retired Police Dog Dies; Was Known for Courage," *Memphis Commercial Appeal,* June 24, 2009.

3. Ibid.

4. Henry Stuttley, "For the Love of Lucy: Oak Brook Man Details Courage of Dog in New Book," *Arlington Heights Daily Herald* (IL), December 7, 2001.

5. Ibid.

6. Garber, *Dog Love,* p. 15.

7. Helton, *Canine Ergonomics,* pp. 4–5.

8. Diana Schaub, "Heroism Goes to the Dogs," *American Enterprise,* September 1, 2000.

9. Vicki Hearne, *Adam's Task: Calling Animals by Name* (New York: Skyhorse Publishing, 2007), p. 22.

10. Sgt. Luther L. Boothe Jr., "Military Working Dogs Join TF Currahee in Afghanistan," DVIDSHub, February 3, 2011.

11. Helen Turner, "Twister the Dog Helps Conservationists with Bat Mystery," *Wales on Sunday,* November 21, 2010.

12. Elaine Marsilio, "Cairn Terrier Helps Search for Turtle Nests," *Corpus Christi Caller-Times,* April 28, 2009.

13. Allen Goldblatt, Irit Gazit, and Joseph Terkel, "Olfaction and Explosives Detector Dogs," in Helton, *Canine Ergonomics,* pp. 137, 142.

14. "Finding Too-Small-to-See Bedbugs No Problem for These Sniffers," U.S. Federal News Service, May 2, 2007.

15. Burkhard Bilger, "Beware of the Dogs," *New Yorker,* February 27, 2012.

16. Tonya Root, "Police Canines Sniff Out Arson and Explosives in Myrtle Beach Area," *Sun News,* May 17, 2010.

17. Bilger, "Beware of the Dogs."

18. Ibid.

19. Louise Miller, "Dogs Teach Humans New Tricks: Extension School Psych Class Fetches Lots of Students," Harvard University *Gazette,* December 8, 2005.

20. Schaub, "Heroism Goes to the Dogs."

21. Clare Howard, "Giant Schnauzer Has

Nose for Mold," *Southtown Star,* May 11, 2008.

22. William S. Helton, Paul J. Feltovich, and Andrew J. Velkey, "Skill and Expertise in Working Dogs: A Cognitive Science Perspective," in Helton, *Canine Ergonomics,* p. 24.

23. William S. Helton, Ph.D., "Canine Ergonomics, Introduction to the New Science of Working Dogs," ibid., p. 5.

24. Jennifer Mertens, "When You Pass Go, Collect $200: Cadaver Dogs Are an Important Tool for Law Enforcement," *Law Enforcement Technology,* July 1, 2005.

25. Sarah Yang, "Wildlife Biologists Put Dogs' Scat-Sniffing Talents to Good Use," U.S. Federal News Service, January 11, 2011.

26. Mehus-Roe, *Working Dogs,* pp. 10, 8.

27. Cathy Newman, "The Dog Whisperer Speaks Out," *National Geographic Cats and Dogs: Celebrating Our Best Friends,* Spring 2012.

28. Rachel Saslow, "Low-Level Aides; in the Halls of Congress, the Pitter-Patter of Paws Lightens the Tension of Governing," *Washington Post,* June 19, 2010.

29. Julie Rovner, "Pet Therapy: How Animals and Humans Heal Each Other," *Morning Edition,* National Public Radio, March 5, 2012.

30. Ibid.
31. Schaub, "Heroism Goes to the Dogs."

Chapter Two: Police Dogs

1. C. R. Sanders, "The Dog You Deserve," *Journal of Contemporary Ethnography* 35, 2006, p. 167.
2. Richard Beene, "Best Weapon in Drug War May Be Man's Best Friend," *Los Angeles Times,* March 3, 1990.
3. Ken Sweet, "Miko's Death a Lesson in Police Dogs' Merits," *Arizona Daily Star,* June 2, 2006.
4. Bob Shaw, "They Fight Crime, but Not for Free," *Saint Paul Pioneer Press,* September 9, 2007.
5. Ibid.
6. Sweet, "Miko's Death a Lesson in Police Dogs' Merits."
7. P. J. Reilly, "Mismatch: Prison Dog Vs. Reporter," *Lancaster Intelligencer Journal/New Era,* October 12, 2011.
8. Walton, *Badge on My Collar.*
9. Burkhard Bilger, "Beware of the Dogs," *New Yorker,* February 27, 2012.
10. Ibid.
11. Ibid.
12. Ibid.
13. Army Sgt. LeeAnn Lloyd, "Canines Remain 'Man's Best Friend' in Fight Against

Terror," DVIDSHub, March 15, 2007.

14. Ricci Graham, "County Sheriffs Going to the Dogs," *Oakland Tribune,* June 5, 2006.

15. Travis M. Whitehead, "Diverse Breeds Work as Police Dogs in the Valley," *McAllen Monitor,* July 30, 2006.

16. Bilger, "Beware of the Dogs."

17. Graham, "County Sheriffs Going to the Dogs."

18. Spc. Jonathan Montgomery, "Bomb Dogs: Guardians of the Gate," DVIDSHub, January 10, 2005.

19. 2nd Lt. Anthony Buchanan, "Dog Days in Iraq," DVIDSHub, January 9, 2006.

20. Reilly, "Mismatch."

21. Buchanan, "Dog Days in Iraq."

22. Bilger, "Beware of the Dogs."

23. Shaw, "They Fight Crime, but Not for Free."

24. "Northumbria Police Dog 'Scared of Children,'" BBC, July 20, 2011.

Chapter Three: Fire Dogs

1. Kim Norvell, "Fire Dog to Sniff Out Possible Arsons," *St. Joseph News-Press,* March 14, 2011.

2. Ann S. Kim, "Arson Dogs Keep Noses Up to Sniff: The Canines and Their Handlers Gather at a Training Facility in Yarmouth to Test Their Skills and Get

Recertified," *Portland Press Herald,* July 21, 2010.

3. "Fire Department Demos Arson Dog," U.S. Federal News Service, July 14, 2008.

4. Tonya Root, "Police Canines Sniff Out Arson and Explosives in Myrtle Beach Area," *Sun News,* May 17, 2010.

5. Kim Norvell, "New Canine Ready to Sniff Out Arson," *St. Joseph News-Press,* October 7, 2011.

6. Lori Chordas, "No Bones About It: State Farm's Arson Dog Program Trains and Funds Accelerant-Detection Dogs to Sniff Out Fraud," *Best's Review,* November 1, 2011.

7. "My Life as a Dog," arsondog.org.

8. Alta Rancho Pet Memorial page, alta-ranchopet.com/memorial.htm.

9. Norvell, "New Canine Ready to Sniff Out Arson."

10. Wendy Leung, "Investigator's Retirement Ends Arson Dogs' Careers," *Inland Valley Daily Bulletin,* August 1, 2009.

11. Gary Taylor, "After 11 Years of Fire Service, Maxine Is Ready to Lead a Dog's Life," *Orlando Sentinel,* June 2, 2011.

Chapter Four: Search-and Rescue Dogs

1. "Canine Disaster Search Team Finds Three Children Alive Under the Rubble,"

Health & Medicine Week, February 1, 2010.

2. Ibid.

3. Marie Peck, Fetch Foundation, e-mail interview, February 20, 2012.

4. Doug Brunk, "The Rest of Your Life: Search and Rescue with a K-9 Nose," *Skin & Allergy News,* February 1, 2010.

5. Sarah Elizabeth Villicana, "Rescue Personnel Honored by Local Organization Sunday," *Porterville Recorder,* March 5, 2007.

6. Brunk, "The Rest of Your Life."

7. Stephanie Bouchard, "Getting a Line on What Goes into K-9 Search, Rescue," *Portland Press Herald,* May 19, 2005.

8. Rebecca Jones, "Search-Rescue Dogs, Handlers Answer Call of the Wilderness," *Rocky Mountain News,* October 25, 2004.

9. Laura A. Bischoff, "Search Dogs Part of Irene Rescue Team," *Dayton Daily News,* August 30, 2011.

10. Ibid.

11. Aimee Hurt and Deborah A. Smith, "Conservation Dogs," in Helton, *Canine Ergonomics,* p. 187.

12. Alexander Ferworn, "Canine Augmentation Technology for Urban Search and Rescue," ibid., p. 219.

13. Hurt and Smith, "Conservation Dogs," p. 185.

14. "Canine's Role in Urban Search and Rescue," www.fema.gov/emergency/usr/canine.shtm.
15. Andrea Bennett, "Highland Woman Has Gone from Teaching to Training Obedience and Search Techniques," *San Bernardino County Sun,* July 6, 2006.
16. "Canine's Role in Urban Search and Rescue."
17. Bennett, "Highland Woman Has Gone from Teaching to Training Obedience and Search Techniques."
18. Bouchard, "Getting a Line on What Goes into K-9 Search, Rescue."
19. Mehus-Roe, *Working Dogs,* p. 203.
20. Jennifer Mertens, "When You Pass Go, Collect $200: Cadaver Dogs Are an Important Tool for Law Enforcement," *Law Enforcement Technology,* July 1, 2005.
21. Ibid.
22. Ibid.

Chapter Five: Guide, Service, and Assistance Dogs

1. Davis and Bunnell, *Working Like Dogs.*
2. Melissa Fay Greene, "Wonder Dog," *New York Times Magazine,* February 2, 2012.
3. "ADA Business BRIEF: Service Animals," April 26, 2002, www.ada.gov

/svcanimb.htm.

4. Donna M. Jackson, *Hero Dogs* (Boston: Little, Brown, 2003), p. 10.

5. Service Dog Central, "What Is the Difference Between a Psychiatric Service Dog and an Emotional Support Animal?" www .servicedogcentral.org/content/node/76. (from April 29, 2004, conference).

6. Beth Landman, "Wagging the Dog, and a Finger," *New York Times,* May 14, 2006.

7. Service Dog Central, "What Is the Difference Between a Psychiatric Service Dog and an Emotional Support Animal?"

8. Ibid.

9. Ilene Springer, "Dogs Helping People: Psychiatric-Service Dogs Are Helping People with Mental Health Problems Live More Normal, Fulfilling Lives," *Dog Watch,* September 1, 2008.

10. "ADA Business BRIEF: Service Animals."

11. Davis and Bunnell, *Working Like Dogs.*

12. Paul Ainsworth, "Training a 'Best Friend' for Their Lifetime of Care," *Brentwood Gazette* (U.K.), July 20, 2011.

13. Greg Botonis, "Four-Footed Helpers: Guide Dogs in Training Meet Kids Who May Own Them," *Los Angeles Daily News,* April 3, 2005.

14. Nancy A. Fischer, "Some Dogs Make

a Life Assisting Those Who Need a Little Help," *Buffalo News,* March 17, 2002.

15. Greene, "Wonder Dog."

16. Ibid.

17. Janie Lorber, "For the Battle-Scarred, Comfort at Leash's End," *New York Times,* April 3, 2010.

18. Marcie Davis and Melissa Bunnell, "Working Like Dogs, Davis Describes a 'Whole New World' After Ramona's Arrival in 1993," *Paraplegia News,* June 1, 2007.

19. Davis and Bunnell, *Working Like Dogs.*

Chapter Six: Therapy Dogs

1. Christine Soares, "Pet Therapy: Huggable Healthcare Workers," *Discovery Health,* December 2011.

2. Florence Nightingale, *Notes on Nursing* (New York: D. Appleton, 1860), p. 103.

3. Dennis Thompson, "The New Face of Pet Therapy," *U.S. News & World Report,* December 27, 2011.

4. James A. Serpell, "Animal-Assisted Interventions in Historical Perspective," in Aubrey H. Fine, ed., *Handbook on Animal Assisted Therapy* (San Diego, CA: Academic Press, 2010), p. 25.

5. Toni Coleman, "Therapy Goes to the Dogs: Group Trains Pets to Fill Support

Roles in Hospitals, Nursing Homes," *Dayton Daily News,* July 28, 2005.

6. Ibid.

7. Rachel Baruch Yackley, "When a Pet Is More than a Pet: Dogs, Cats, Birds, Even a Rabbit, Have Jobs to Do at Nursing Homes," *Daily Herald* (Arlington Heights, IL), September 20, 2002.

8. Pat Pheifer, "Prisoners Paw It Forward," *Star Tribune,* January 10, 2010.

9. Thompson, "The New Face of Pet Therapy."

10. Rivera, *On Dogs and Dying,* p. 7.

11. Ibid.

12. "Certified Therapy Dog Helps Patients in Speech, Physical, and Occupational Therapy at Community Hospital," www.comhs.org, March 27, 2007.

13. Carol Rock, "Recovery Rx: Bit of Slobber, Smile and Wag. Bedside Dog Therapists Soothe Hospital Patients," *Los Angeles Daily News,* January 15, 2006.

14. Ibid.

15. Rebecca Jones, "Animal Therapists Provide Solace, Training," EdNews Colorado.org, December 23, 2010.

16. Ibid.

17. Jamie Kelly, "Scout the Lab Helps Children with Speech Difficulties, Special Needs," *Missoulian,* May 23, 2011.

18. Iris Campbell, "Animal Reading Friends Help Boost Travis Students' Reading Skills," *San Marcos Daily Record,* March 8, 2011.

19. Levinson, *Pets and Human Development,* pp. 6, xiv.

20. Melinda Beck, "The Doctor's Dog Will See You Now," *Wall Street Journal,* December 20, 2010.

21. Ibid.

22. Thompson, "The New Face of Pet Therapy."

23. Maryann Mott, "Comfort Dogs Come to Emotional Rescue; Specially Trained Canines Help Those Suffering Aftermath of Disaster, Having Daily Struggles," *HealthDay News,* March 18, 2010.

24. Jan Pudlow, " 'Low-Tech and High-Touch': Pet Therapy in the Courts Is a New Tool for Victims," *Florida Bar News,* March 15, 2010.

25. Ibid.

26. "Therapy Dog Takes Edge off Law Exams," Associated Press, December 18, 2011.

27. Ashley J. Cerasaro, "Four-Legged Therapists," *New Jersey Monthly,* October 10, 2011.

28. Ibid.

29. Ibid.

30. "How to Become a Registered Therapy Team," PetPartners.org.

31. Team Evaluation, PetPartners.org.

32. Soares, "Pet Therapy."

33. Cerasaro, "Four-Legged Therapists."

34. Ellen Michaud, "Therapy Dogs and Healing," *Saturday Evening Post,* November/December 2011.

35. Ibid.

36. Pudlow, " 'Low-Tech and High-Touch.' "

Chapter Seven: Prison Dogs

1. Makos and Solberg, *Puppies Behind Bars,* p. 14.

2. Gennifer Furst, William Paterson University, e-mail interview, March 12, 2012.

3. "Prison Dog Training Program Celebrating Third Anniversary and Graduation Ceremony for Latest Canine Class," States News Service, June 28, 2010.

4. Ibid.

5. Andrea Neal, "Trained Dogs Transforming Lives," *Saturday Evening Post,* September 1, 2005.

6. Rick Armon, "This Prison Program Is for the Dogs," *Akron Beacon Journal,* November 24, 2006.

7. Pat Pheifer, "Prisoners Paw It Forward," *Minneapolis Star Tribune,* January 10, 2010.

8. Neal, "Trained Dogs Transforming Lives."

9. Marjorie Coeyman, "New Leash on Life," *Christian Science Monitor,* August 16, 2000.

10. Armon, "This Prison Program Is for the Dogs."

11. Ibid.

12. Kevin McKenzie, "Ready to Nurture — Inmates Looking to Collierville Animal Services to Revive Prison's Dog Program," *Memphis Commercial Appeal,* September 8, 2008.

13. Coeyman, "New Leash on Life."

14. Armon, "This Prison Program Is for the Dogs."

15. Coeyman, "New Leash on Life."

16. Mehus-Roe, *Working Dogs,* p. 99.

17. Pheifer, "Prisoners Paw It Forward."

Chapter Eight: Medical-Detection Dogs

1. Jenny Stocks, "The Dogs That Can Detect Cancer: Meet the Four-Legged 'Bio-Detectives' Who Are Pioneering a Health Revolution," *Daily Mail* (London), November 16, 2011.

2. "Dogs Smell Diabetic Attacks Coming," NationalGeographic.com, June 2, 2009.

3. Ibid.

4. Sarah Moses, "Trained to Be on Alert: Dogs Can Sense a Diabetic's Blood Sugar

Changes, Warn Families," *Syracuse Post-Standard,* February 12, 2012.

5. Sandra J. Pennecke, "A Service Dog Could Be a Little Girl's, and Her Family's, Best Friend," *Virginian-Pilot,* November 21, 2010.

6. Tom Rademacher, "Dog Eats Rockford Man's Big Toe, Saves His Life," *Grand Rapids Press,* August 3, 2010.

7. Brian Newsome, "Peanut-Sniffing Dog Is Allergic Girl's Best Friend," *Colorado Springs Gazette,* February 17, 2009.

8. Ibid.

9. Celeste Busk, "Family Relies on Seizure Dog for Children's Safety," *Chicago Sun-Times,* June 23, 2009.

10. Ibid.

11. Ibid.

12. Christine Kellett, "Dog Given Medal After 'Canine CPR,'" *Brisbane Times,* October 28, 2009.

13. Melissa Thompson, "Dog That Won't Let Sleeping Girls Lie; Pooch Is a Lifesaver," *Mirror* (London), June 6, 2011.

14. Andy Dolan, "Saved by the Dog-tor," *Daily Mail* (London), February 27, 2009.

15. Lin Jenkins, "How the 'Bio-Detective' Dogs Can Sniff Out Cancer," *Mail on Sunday* (London), March 2, 2008.

16. Jordan E. Rosenfeld, "You Unlucky

Dog," *Pacific Sun,* April 13, 2007.
17. Jenkins, "How the 'Bio-Detective' Dogs Can Sniff Out Cancer."

Chapter Nine: Wildlife-Detection and -Conservation Dogs

1. Susan Milius, "Hey, What About Us? There's More Life on Ice than Celebrity Bears," *Science News,* December 1, 2007.
2. "Wildlife Biologists Put Dogs' Scat-Sniffing Talents to Good Use," U.S. Federal News Service, January 11, 2011.
3. Ibid.
4. Ibid.
5. Ibid.
6. Kenneth R. Weiss, "A Nose for Wild Things," *Los Angeles Times,* November 13, 2010.
7. Kirsten Weir, "Dog Chases Whale Scat," *Scientist,* August 1, 2006.
8. Judith Lavoie, "Dog's Nose for Whale Poop Big Help to B.C. Orca Researchers," Canwest News Service, November 20, 2008.
9. Taryn Luntz, "Dog Provides Low-Cost, Low-Tech Fix for Cities' Sewer Problems," *Greenwire/New York Times,* August 18, 2009.
10. Jonathan Serrie, "Man's Best Friend Thwarts Environmental Enemies in

the Florida Everglades," FoxNews.com, March 1, 2012.

11. "A Giant Battle: Auburn Canines Help in Search for Everglades' Pythons," States News Service, February 9, 2012.

12. Becky Bohrer, "Can Dogs Sniff Out Noxious Weeds?" *Deseret News,* December 25, 2003.

13. Tim Tesconi, "Dogs Sniffing Out Pest on Grapevines," *Press Democrat,* February 26, 2006.

14. Jerry Jackson, "Detection Dogs Show Promise in Sniffing Out Pests," *Citrus + Vegetable,* February 10, 2012.

15. Andrew N. Guthrie, "Dog Helps Save Sea Turtles," *The Bark,* May/June 2009.

16. Dean Fosdick, "Poachers Steal Public Plants; Collectors Join Other Thieves in Endangering Beneficial Wildlife," *Columbian* (Vancouver, WA), June 5, 2002.

17. Matt Ehlers, "Pest-Sniffing Canines Hunt Bedbugs, Termites," *Raleigh News and Observer,* April 28, 2010.

18. Allison Aubrey, "The Only Good Bedbug Is a Toasty One," *All Things Considered,* National Public Radio, April 14, 2009.

19. Lena H. Sun, "Dogs That Sniff Out Bedbugs in Demand," *Washington Post,* May 29, 2011.

20. "Finding Too-Small-to-See Bedbugs No Problem for These Sniffers," U.S. Federal News Service, May 2, 2007.

21. Sun, "Dogs That Sniff Out Bedbugs in Demand."

22. Anne Marie Fuller, "Mold Detecting Tracy Terrier," *Oakland Tribune,* February 11, 2011.

23. Clare Howard, "Giant Schnauzer Has Nose for Mold," *Southtown Star,* May 11, 2008.

24. Andrew Forgrave, "One Sniff and He's Off Saving Nature," *Daily Post/Liverpool,* January 6, 2011.

Chapter Ten: Civilian Dogs

1. "Good Dog! Toby Saves His Owner," *Memphis Commercial Appeal,* November 3, 2007.

2. "Dog Saves Choking Owner with 'Heimlich,'" AP Online, March 28, 2007.

3. Clifford Davis, "Dog-Bite Victim, Dog-Shot Victim Recovering Together in Jacksonville," *Florida Times-Union,* June 10, 2011.

4. Erin Hawley, "Strutt Your Mutt: Shot, Paralyzed Dog Running Again with Heroes' Help," *Jacksonville First Coast News,* September 21, 2011.

5. Laura T. Coffey, "Deformed Puppy,

Rescued from Trash, Learns to Walk," MSNBC.com, September 23, 2011.

6. Laura T. Coffey, "Harper the Once-Deformed Puppy Is Doing Great — and Doing Lots of Good, Too," MSNBC.com, March 12, 2012.

7. Tatiana Pina, "Owner Recalls Impact of RISPCA's Canine Ambassador," *Providence Journal,* January 21, 2010.

8. Ibid.

9. Corey Van't Haaff, "An Amazing Two-Legged Dog Provides Hope and Inspiration," *Modern Dog Magazine,* May 2011.

10. Ibid.

11. Sue Manning, "Two-Legged Dog Helps Inspire Others: Canine Makes Dozens of Stops Each Year," *Charleston Daily Mail,* December 17, 2009.

12. Ibid.

13. Rhiannon Ross, "Home Sweet Home: Shelter to Welcome Victims' Pets," *Her Magazine, Kansas City,* January 2012.

14. "Rose Brooks Center Commended for Protecting People and Pets," States News Service, March 16, 2012.

15. Sonia Moghe, "Dog Saves Woman's Life, Being Honored Today," WGCL-TV, October 23, 2011.

16. Nick Pisa, "Abandoned Dog Found Whimpering in Snowy Alps by Rescue

Team After Ten-Day Search in −10C Temperatures," *Daily Mail* (London), February 7, 2012.

17. Russell Lissau, "Persistent Dog Helps Save Woman Who Fell into River Just Outside of Libertyville," *Arlington Heights Daily Herald,* January 2, 1998.

Chapter Eleven: Celebrity Dogs of Courage

1. Diana Schaub, "Heroism Goes to the Dogs," *American Enterprise,* September 1, 2000.
2. Javna, *Animal Superstars,* p. 58.
3. Ketzel Levine, "The Man Behind Lassie's On-Screen Magic," *Morning Edition,* National Public Radio, September 8, 2006.
4. Roger Moore, "'Marley' Trainer Wrangles 22 Dogs in Roles as Movie Namesake," *Pittsburgh Tribune-Review,* December 30, 2008.
5. Cristy Lytal, "*Marley* Minds Its Pees and Cues," *Los Angeles Times,* December 28, 2008.
6. Moore, "'Marley' Trainer Wrangles 22 Dogs in Roles as Movie Namesake."
7. Lytal, "*Marley* Minds Its Pees and Cues."
8. Janet Weeks, "Homeward Bow-wownd: For Trainer, It Was More Than the Usual Fur-Flying Tail of Bickering Co-Stars,"

Daily News Los Angeles, March 12, 1996.

9. Orlean, *Rin Tin Tin,* p. 3.

10. Scott Simon, "Talks with Lassie's Trainer and Smokey's Creator," *Weekend Edition,* National Public Radio, August 6, 1994.

11. Bob Thomas, "Lassie: Loyal for 50 Years: Canine Icon That Went from Big Screen to TV Is One of World's Most Beloved Pets," *Columbian* (Vancouver, WA), October 3, 2004.

12. Ibid.

13. Ibid.

14. Daniel Ruth, "Disney's *Old Yeller* Still Teaches a Hard Lesson," *Chicago Sun-Times,* June 5, 1986.

15. Ibid.

16. Moore, "'Marley' Trainer Wrangles 22 Dogs in Roles as Movie Namesake."

RESOURCES

Books

American Rescue Dog Association. *Search and Rescue Dogs: Training the K-9 Hero.* New York: Howell Book House, 2002.

Anderson, Allen, and Linda Anderson, eds. *Angel Dogs: Divine Messengers of Love.* Novato, CA: New World Library, 2005.

————. *Angel Dogs with a Mission: Divine Messengers in Service to All Life.* Novato, CA: New World Library, 2008.

Arnold, Caroline. *A Guide Dog Puppy Grows Up.* San Diego: Harcourt, 1991.

Arnold, Jennifer. *In a Dog's Heart: What Our Dogs Need, Want, and Deserve — and the Gifts We Can Expect in Return.* New York: Spiegel & Grau, 2011.

————. *Through a Dog's Eyes: Understanding Our Dogs by Understanding How They See the World.* New York: Spiegel & Grau, 2010.

Ascarelli, Miriam. *Independent Vision: Dorothy Harrison Eustis and the Story of the Seeing*

Eye. West Lafayette, IN: Purdue University Press, 2010.

Bare, Colleen Stanley. *Sammy, Dog Detective.* New York: Dutton, 1998.

Bauer, Nona Kilgore. *Dog Heroes of September 11th: A Tribute to America's Search and Rescue Dogs.* 10th anniversary ed. Freehold, NJ: Kennel Club Books, 2011.

Beck, Ken, and Jim Clark. *The Encyclopedia of TV Pets: A Complete History of Television's Greatest Animal Stars.* Nashville: Rutledge Hill Press, 2002.

Bidner, Jen. *Dog Heroes: Saving Lives and Protecting America.* Guilford, CT: Lyons Press, 2006.

Bozzo, Linda. *Fire Dog Heroes: Amazing Working Dogs with American Humane.* Berkeley Heights, NJ: Enslow, 2011.

Bryson, Sandy. *Police Dog Tactics.* New York: McGraw-Hill, 1996.

Bulanda, Susan. *Ready! Training the Search and Rescue Dog.* 2nd ed. Freehold, NJ: Kennel Club Books, 2010.

Burch, Mary R. *Volunteering with Your Pet: How to Get Involved in Animal-Assisted Therapy with Any Kind of Pet.* New York: Howell Book House, 1996.

Butler, Kris. *Therapy Dogs Today: Their Gifts, Our Obligation.* Norman, OK: Funpuddle Publishing, 2004.

Calmenson, Stephanie. *Rosie, a Visiting Dog's Story.* New York: Clarion Books, 1994.

Chapman, Samuel G. *Police Dogs in North America.* Springfield, IL: Charles C. Thomas, 1990.

Charleson, Susannah. *Scent of the Missing: Love and Partnerships with a Search-and-Rescue Dog.* Boston: Houghton Mifflin Harcourt, 2010.

Collins, Ace. *Lassie: A Dog's Life: The First Fifty Years.* New York: Penguin, 1993.

Coren, Stanley. *The Intelligence of Dogs: A Guide to the Thoughts, Emotions, and Inner Lives of Our Canine Companions.* New York: Free Press, 2005.

Crawford, Jacqueline J., and Karen A. Pomerinke. *Therapy Pets: The Animal-Human Healing Partnership.* Amherst, NY: Prometheus Books, 2003.

Davis, Kathy Diamond. *Therapy Dogs: Training Your Dog to Help Others.* Wenatchee, WA: Dogwise Publishing, 2002.

Davis, Marcie, and Melissa Bunnell. *Working Like Dogs: The Service Dog Guidebook.* Crawford, CO: Alpine Publications, 2007.

Dibra, Bash, with Kitty Brown. *StarPet: How to Make Your Pet a Star.* New York: Pocket Books, 2005.

Eames, Ed, and Toni Eames. *Partners in Independence: A Success Story of Dogs and the Disabled.* Mechanicsburg, PA: Barkleigh Productions, 2004.

Edelson, Edward. *Great Animals of the Movies.* Garden City, NY: Doubleday, 1980.

Eden, R. S. *K9 Officer's Manual.* Bellingham, WA: Temeron Books, 1993.

Farran, Christopher. *Dogs on the Job! True Stories of Phenomenal Dogs.* New York: Avon Books, 2003.

Fetty, Margaret. *Seizure-Alert Dogs: Dog Heroes.* New York: Bearport Publishing, 2010.

Fine, Aubrey H., ed. *Handbook on Animal-Assisted Therapy: Theoretical Foundations and Guidelines for Practice.* 3rd ed. Burlington, MA: Academic Press, 2010.

Frank, Morris, and Blake Clark. *First Lady of the Seeing Eye.* New York: Holt, 1966.

Frei, David. *Angel on a Leash: Therapy Dogs and the Lives They Touch.* Irvine, CA: BowTie Press, 2011.

Furst, Gennifer. *Animal Programs in Prison: A Comprehensive Assessment.* Boulder, CO: FirstForumPress, 2011.

Garber, Marjorie. *Dog Love.* New York: Touchstone, 1997.

Goldish, Meish. *Bomb-Sniffing Dogs.* New York: Bearport Publishing, 2012.

———. *Hollywood Dogs.* New York: Bearport Publishing, 2007.

————. *Pest-Sniffing Dogs*. New York: Bearport Publishing, 2012.

Gorrell, Gena K. *Working Like a Dog: The Story of Working Dogs Through History*. Plattsburgh, NY: Tundra Books, 2003.

Grandin, Temple, and Catherine Johnson. *Animals Make Us Human: Creating the Best Life for Animals*. Boston: Houghton Mifflin Harcourt, 2009.

Greenberg, Dan. *Wilderness Search Dogs*. New York: Bearport Publishing, 2005.

Grover, Stacy. *101 Creative Ideas for Animal Assisted Therapy*. Henderson, NV: Motivational Press, 2010.

Helfer, Ralph. *The Beauty of the Beasts: Tales of Hollywood's Animal Stars*. New York: Harper, 2007.

Helton, William S., ed. *Canine Ergonomics: The Science of Working Dogs*. Boca Raton, FL: CRC Press, 2009.

Hingson, Michael, with Susy Flory. *Thunder Dog: The True Story of a Blind Man, His Guide Dog, and the Triumph of Trust at Ground Zero*. Nashville: Thomas Nelson, 2011.

Javna, John. *Animal Superstars*. Milwaukee: Hal Leonard Books, 1986.

Jones, Peter C., and Lisa MacDonald. *Hero Dogs: 100 True Stories of Daring Deeds*. Kansas City, MO: Andrews and McMeel, 1997.

Judah, Christy. *Water Search: Search and Rescue Dogs Finding Drowned Persons.* CreateSpace, 2011.

Judah, J. C. *Buzzards and Butterflies: Human Remains Detection Dogs.* Wilmington, NC: Coastal Books, 2008.

Kehret, Peg. *Shelter Dogs: Amazing Stories of Adopted Strays.* Morton Grove, IL: Albert Whitman, 1999.

Koontz, Dean. *A Big Little Life: A Memoir of a Joyful Dog.* New York: Hyperion, 2009.

Latham, Donna. *Fire Dogs.* New York: Bearport Publishing, 2006.

Leder, Jane Mersky. *Stunt Dogs.* Mankato, MN: Crestwood House, 1985.

Levinson, Boris M. *Pets and Human Development.* Springfield, IL: Charles C. Thomas, 1972.

Lind, Nancy. *Animal Assisted Therapy Activities to Motivate and Inspire.* Lombard, IL: Pyow Sports Marketing, 2009.

Lufkin, Elise. *To the Rescue: Found Dogs with a Mission.* New York: Skyhorse Publishing, 2009.

Makos, Christopher, and Paul Solberg. *Puppies Behind Bars: Training Puppies to Change Lives.* New York: Glitterati Incorporated, 2007.

McCarthy, Meghan. *The Incredible Life of Balto.* New York: Knopf, 2011.

McDaniel, Melissa. *Disaster Search Dogs.* New York: Bearport Publishing, 2005.

———. *Guide Dogs.* New York: Bearport Publishing, 2005.

McPherson, Rachel. *Every Dog Has a Gift: True Stories of Dogs Who Bring Hope and Healing into Our Lives.* New York: Jeremy Tarcher, 2010.

Mehus-Roe, Kristin. *Working Dogs: True Stories of Dogs and Their Handlers.* Irvine, CA: BowTie Press, 2003.

Meyer, Karl. *Dog Heroes: Tales of Dramatic Rescues, Courageous Journeys, and True-Blue Friendships.* North Adams, MA: Storey Publishing, 2008.

Moose, with Brian Hargrove. *My Life as a Dog.* New York: Harper, 2000.

Murphy, Claire Rudolf, and Jane G. Haigh. *Gold Rush Dogs.* Anchorage: Alaska Northwest Books, 2001.

O'Neill, Catherine. *Dogs on Duty.* Washington, D.C.: National Geographic Society, 1988.

Orlean, Susan. *Rin Tin Tin: The Life and the Legend.* New York: Simon & Schuster, 2011.

Orsinger, Trevor J., and Drew F. Orsinger. *The Firefighter's Best Friend: Lives and Legends of Chicago Firehouse Dogs.* Chicago: Lake Claremont Press, 2003.

Osborne, Mary Pope, and Natalie Pope Boyce. *Dog Heroes: Magic Tree House Fact Tracker #24: Dog Heroes: A Nonfiction Companion to Magic Tree House #46: Dogs in the Dead of Night.* New York: Random House, 2011.

Owens, Carrie. *Working Dogs.* Rocklin, CA: Prima Publishing, 1999.

Paietta, Ann C., and Jean L. Kauppila. *Animals on Screen and Radio: An Annotated Sourcebook.* Metuchen, NJ: Scarecrow Press, 1994.

Painter, Deborah. *Hollywood's Top Dogs: The Dog Hero in Film.* Baltimore: Midnight Marquee Press, 2008.

Pichot, Teri, and Marc Coulter. *Animal-Assisted Brief Therapy: A Solution-Focused Approach.* Binghamton, NY: Haworth Press, 2007.

Presnall, Judith Janda. *Animal Actors: Animals with Jobs.* San Diego: KidHaven Press, 2002.

Rebmann, Andrew J., Edward David, and Marcella H. Sorg. *Cadaver Dog Handbook: Forensic Training and Tactics for the Recovery of Human Remains.* Boca Raton, FL: CRC Press, 2000.

Rivera, Michelle A. *Canines in the Classroom: Raising Humane Children Through Interactions with Animals.* New York: Lantern Books, 2004.

————. *On Dogs and Dying: Inspirational Stories from Hospice Hounds.* West Lafayette, IN: Purdue University Press, 2010.

Rosenthal, Richard. *K-9 Cops: Stories from America's K-9 Police Units.* New York: Pocket Books, 1997.

Rothel, David. *The Great Show Business Animals.* San Diego: A. S. Barnes, 1980.

Ruffin, Frances E. *Medical Detective Dogs.* New York: Bearport Publishing, 2007.

————. *Police Dogs.* New York: Bearport Publishing, 2005.

————. *Water Rescue Dogs.* New York: Bearport Publishing, 2006.

Sakson, Sharon. *Paws & Effect: The Healing Power of Dogs.* New York: Spiegel & Grau, 2009.

Sanders, Clinton R. *Understanding Dogs: Living and Working with Canine Companions.* Philadelphia: Temple University Press, 1999.

Silverman, Maida. *Snow Search Dogs.* New York: Bearport Publishing, 2005.

Silverman, Stephen M. *Movie Mutts: Hollywood Goes to the Dogs.* New York: Harry N. Abrams, 2001.

Singer, Marilyn. *A Dog's Gotta Do What a Dog's Gotta Do.* New York: Henry Holt, 2000.

Somerville, Bob. *Dogtown: A Sanctuary for Rescued Dogs.* South Portland, ME: Sellers Publishing, 2008.

Stamper, Judith Bauer. *Eco Dogs.* New York: Bearport Publishing, 2011.

Steiger, Brad, and Sherry Hansen Steiger. *Dog Miracles: Inspirational and Heroic True Stories.* Holbrook, MA: Adams Media, 2001.

Tagliaferro, Linda. *Service Dogs.* New York: Bearport Publishing, 2005.

Taylor, Jordan. *Wonder Dogs: 101 German Shepherd Dog Films.* Bainbridge Island, WA: Reel Dogs Press, 2009.

VanFleet, Risë. *Play Therapy with Kids and Canines: Benefits for Children's Developmental and Psychosocial Health.* Sarasota, FL: Professional Resource Press, 2008.

Walton, Marilyn Jeffers. *Badge on My Collar: A Chronicle of Courageous Canines.* Bloomington, IN: AuthorHouse, 2007.

———. *Badge on My Collar II: To Serve with Honor.* Bloomington, IN: AuthorHouse, 2009.

Watson, Sam D., Jr. *Dogs for Police Service: Programming and Training.* Springfield, IL: Charles C. Thomas, 1972.

Weatherwax, Rudd B., and John H. Rothwell. *The Story of Lassie: His Discovery and Training from Puppyhood to Stardom.* New

York: Duell, Sloan & Pearce, 1950.

Weisbord, Merrily, and Kim Kachanoff. *Dogs with Jobs: Working Dogs Around the World.* New York: Pocket Books, 2000.

Wilkes, Jane K. *The Role of Companion Animals in Counseling and Psychology: Discovering Their Use in the Therapeutic Process.* Springfield, IL: Charles C. Thomas, 2009.

Organizations

Advanced K9 Detection
www.advancedk9detectives.com

American Humane Association
www.americanhumane.org

American Humane Association Film and Television Unit
www.ahafilm.org

American Rescue Dog Association
www.ardainc.org

American Society for the Prevention of Cruelty to Animals
www.aspca.org

Angel on a Leash
www.angelonaleash.com

Arson Dog
www.arsondog.org

Assistance Dog Institute
www.assistancedog.org

Assistance Dogs International
www.adionline.org

Cadaver Dogs
www.cadaverdog.com

Canadian Avalanche Rescue Dog Association
www.carda.bc.ca/

Canine Assistants
www.canineassistants.org

Canine Companions for Independence
www.cci.org

Center for Conservation Biology
www.conservationbiology.net

Disaster Dog
www.disasterdog.org

Dogs for the Deaf
www.dogsforthedeaf.org

Federal Emergency Management Administration
www.fema.gov

4 Paws for Ability, Inc.
www.4pawsforability.org

Gabriel's Angels
www.gabrielsangels.org

Good Dog Foundation
www.thegooddogfoundation.org

Guide Dog Foundation for the Blind
www.guidedog.org

Guide Dogs for the Blind
www.guidedogs.com

Guide Dogs of America
www.guidedogsofamerica.org

Guiding Eyes for the Blind
www.guidingeyes.org

Happy Tails Service Dogs
www.happytailsservicedogs.com

Healing Species
www.healingspecies.org

Humane Society of the United States
www.hsus.org

Intermountain Therapy Animals
www.therapyanimals.org

International Association of Assistance Dog
Partners
www.iaadp.org

International Hearing Dog, Inc.
www.hearingdog.org

International Police K9 Conferences
www.policek9.com

National Animal Assisted Crisis Response
www.animalassistedcrisisresponse.org

National Association for Search and Rescue
www.nasar.org

National Disaster Search Dog Foundation
www.ndsdf.org

National Education for Assistance Dog Services
www.neads.org

National Police Canine Association
www.npca.net

National Urban Search and Rescue Response System
www.fema.gov/usr

North American Police Work Dog Association
www.napwda.com

Northwest Disaster Search Dogs
www.ndsd.net

Paws for Comfort
www.pawsforcomfort.com

Paws with a Cause
www.pawswithacause.org

Pet Partners (formerly the Delta Society)
www.petpartersne.org

Police Dog Foundation
www.policedogfoundation.org

Prison Pet Partnership Program
www.prisonpetpartnership.org

Puppies Behind Bars
www.puppiesbehindbars.com

Search Dog Foundation
www.searchdogfoundation.org

Seeing Eye
www.seeingeye.org

Service Dog Academy
www.servicedogacademy.com

Therapy Dogs International
www.tdi-dog.org

United Police & Corrections K-9 Association, Inc.
www.upcka.org

United States Police Canine Association
www.uspcak9.com

Wet Dogs/Water Education and Training Dog Obedience Group
www.polyhedrongroup.com/wetdog/index.html

Working Dogs for Conservation
www.workingdogsforconservation.org

ACKNOWLEDGMENTS

If you look up the term *superagent* in the dictionary, there you will find Scott Mendel's picture.

Thanks also go to Peter Joseph at St. Martin's Press, along with Tom Dunne, Sally Richardson, Matthew Shear, and Margaret Sutherland Brown.

Eternal gratitude to my buddies, who have witnessed me in the throes of producing a book several times over at this point and still willingly put themselves through it: Cheryl Trotta, Dean Hollatz, Leslie Caputo, Michael Murray, John Willson and David Porter, and Bob DiPrete and Reagan, aka Poochie, a Dog of Courage in his own right.

Lastly, kudos to Alex Ishii, whose love and companionship make crazy deadlines a lot easier to endure.

ABOUT THE AUTHOR

Lisa Rogak is author of *The Dogs of War: The Courage, Love, and Loyalty of Military Working Dogs* as well as the Edgar- and Anthony-nominated *Haunted Heart: The Life and Times of Stephen King* and editor of *The New York Times*-bestselling *Barack Obama in His Own Words.*